A Rainbow Book

THE DEBT TRAP

How Your Life Choices Impact on Your Financial Future

STEVEN N. TAIEB

Rainbow Books, Inc.
FLORIDA

Library of Congress Cataloging-in-Publication Data

Taieb, Steven N., 1959-
The debt trap : how your life choices impact on your financial future / by Steven N. Taieb.
p. cm.
Includes bibliographical references and index.
ISBN 1-56825-088-6 (softcover : alk. paper)
1. Finance, Personal. 2. Values. 3. Life. I. Title.

HG179.T37 2003
332.024'02—dc21 2002154808

THE DEBT TRAP
How Traditional Values-Based Choices Can Prevent Debt

ISBN 1-56825-088-6

Published by
Rainbow Books, Inc.
P. O. Box 430
Highland City, FL 33846-0430

Editorial Offices and Wholesale/Distributor Orders
Telephone: (863) 648-4420
Email: RBIbooks@aol.com

Individuals' Orders
Toll-free Telephone (800) 431-1579 • http://www.AllBookStores.com

Reading this book is not a guarantee that you will never get in debt. This book conveys one person's ideas about certain choices and values that may help you avoid debt. If you are looking for a foolproof way of avoiding debt, you should consult your own lawyer to go over your individual circumstances.

First Printing
Printed in the United States of America.

Contents

ACKNOWLEDGMENTS

I would like to thank my wife, Jamie, for her research, encouragement and for the choices she has made to live a life free of debt. Also, kudos to Matthew Goldberg for his research for *The Debt Trap*.

I would never be able to complete this project without the assistance of Gale Ford, who spent hours helping me type and retype the manuscript, and for her encouragement for this project.

I owe a debt of gratitude to my father, Simon Taieb, for teaching me about how the choices you make in life do matter. Also, I can't forget the valuable lessons I learned from my mother, Sandra Taieb, and my grandmother, Charlotte Goodman, of blessed memory.

I finally wish to thank all of my colleagues who have encouraged me to press on with this book while maintaining a full-time, demanding law practice.

Introduction

Why would I write a book about avoiding debt? I have been practicing consumer bankruptcy law for 17 years in New Jersey and Pennsylvania, and I have seen almost every reason why people get into debt. I have made every effort to help people save their property by either reorganizing their debt or helping them get a fresh start.

The biggest problem I have is that, even though the vast majority of the people I have helped are honorable, hard-working people, they have made such crucial mistakes in their life choices that it is difficult to fix some deep-rooted symptoms.

Most people I have dealt with lack any basis of money management. They get into debt because they have a basic misunderstanding of budgeting. Also, certain life choices have created consequences that make it much harder to live debt free.

After meeting with several thousand people over the last 17

years, I have analyzed the reasons why people fell into debt and filed for bankruptcy. In addition, I have done extensive research, which backs up a lot of my theories.

Over the past 17 years I have helped more than 5,000 people who have found themselves in debt, specifically due to the poor choices they have made. Some people end up in debt because of circumstances outside of their control, such as catastrophic illness or misplaced trust in the wrong people. However, if you adhere to certain fundamentals in life, the advice in this book can help you prevent getting into debt just as certain preventive health practices protect you from debilitating diseases.

Too many people graduate high school, college, and even graduate school, without any understanding about budgeting. The American Dream is still alive and well, but most people have little or no knowledge of how to make the choices necessary to live a life free of debt.

Since the media and advertisers hype instant gratification, it is no wonder over one million Americans had to use the bankruptcy process in 1998 to deal with financial problems. What is more amazing is how few Americans truly live a debt-free life — one in which they pay the full balance on their credit card obligations each month and own all their property free and clear.

This book will be a road map to help you avoid life's potential pitfalls. It will encourage you to consider a range of social, moral and practical financial issues that you will face as you grow older.

A major issue that must be considered has to do with your relationships. Whether you have a successful marriage or end up being a single parent is crucial. Are you together with your partner, or are you stuck with a child support obligation that can drain you financially for years to come? Do you make the right choices regarding the person with whom you want to have children and start a family? Life frequently throws you curve balls, and you grow by learning from your mistakes. However, some mistakes make it much harder to get out of the debt trap.

After relationship choices, you must consider conspicuous consumption and the "more is better" mentality. Are you satisfied with your material needs, or do you need to constantly get more material goods and incur more debt to fulfill yourself? Do you, the current generation of young people, understand the notion of savings and sacrifice, or is the media's notion of instant gratification and "you can have it all" influencing your life?

Do you really understand what you are getting into when you decide to purchase a home? Do you correctly anticipate the increased expenses that will come with a larger family? Do you save for a rainy day? Do you rely on the bank's qualification for a mortgage? Do you think through *all* the costs involved with a home?

What about your car? Do you own your car? Do you consider the payments, costs of insurance, repairs and equity? Is personal responsibility alive and well in you? For some people, the social programs — from the New Deal to the Great Society — have made them feel entitled.

This book delves into the historical, social, moral and economic reasons why so many Americans are caught in the debt trap. You will learn what to avoid from the mistakes of others. It will teach you about life, something about which your schools, unfortunately, never trained you.

There are several agencies and many books that deal with people who have amassed large debt and propose plans to eliminate that debt, but they provide assistance only to those who are already in trouble. This book is for the reader who wants to avoid trouble. It will help you rethink a lot of fundamental values and, hopefully, give you the opportunity for a life of real fulfillment in which debt does not exist.

God bless you, and stay the course.

—Steven N. Taieb

Chapter 1

Your Home Is Your Castle

One of the major tenets of the American Dream is that everyone is entitled to home ownership. It is amazing the number of existing mortgage companies that try to get your business. The media constantly reinforces the idea that, pursuant to the American Dream, you too can have your own home. The U.S. Government even subsidizes special agencies to help people purchase their first home. Essentially, when new home construction is good, the economy is good.

It is wonderful for you to be able to own your own home, but home ownership is not for everyone. Your home is going to be the biggest investment you will ever make; therefore, you don't want to purchase a home that will force you into a life of debt.

Naturally, you want to live in a nice home located in a good neighborhood with quality schools for your children. Your financial situation dictates what type of home you can afford. Some mortgage companies use a magical 20 percent down payment formula. However, I have seen clients who have put only a couple of thousand dollars down and have ended up with mortgages that are way over their financial heads.

Don't "Qualify" for Disaster

Unfortunately, too many people listen to mortgage companies. They will frequently qualify you for mortgages that, from the start, put you in a free fall toward foreclosure. It is in the broker's interest to approve you for a mortgage. Also, your realtor wants you to buy the home — no matter what the cost — since he or she gets a commission only if the home is sold. Remember, neither the mortgage broker nor the realtor pays your mortgage; you are the one who is ultimately responsible for making the payment. Many people I see, those who "qualified" for a mortgage, now live from pay check to pay check and have absolutely no savings. In the event of a job loss, illness or accident, the Sheriff will be knocking on their doors.

Why shouldn't you accept a bank's representation that you qualify for a mortgage? Isn't the bank in the business of making these decisions for you? My response is that, in life, there are many intangibles and emergencies that occur that are not anticipated when you are initially screened for a mortgage.

Take the example of Jack and Jill. Jack is a 30-year-old professional who earns $40,000 per year, and Jill is 28 years old and also earns $40,000 per year. Based on the fact that they earned a sizable combined income, they easily qualified for a $150,000 mortgage. Since they put $30,000 down, they purchased a home for $180,000 and had a 30-year mortgage with monthly payments of $998, which included only the principal and interest. Jack and Jill were also responsible for taxes and homeowners insurance, which were not included in the mortgage.

Initially, everything was financially fine for Jack and Jill.

However, within six months of the home purchase, Jack's old car fell apart, so he decided to lease a new vehicle for $399 per month. A year later, Jill felt it was time for her to get a vehicle, so she financed a car at $350 a month for five years. It was a little tighter with the car payments, but they were both doing well on their jobs, and each got modest raises.

Then, Jill got pregnant. This was a new challenge. If Jill stopped working, there would be a substantial drop in the family income; but, if she continued her job, childcare expenses would be astronomical, which would put a dent in Jack and Jill's pocketbook.

Jill eventually quit her job, and credit cards became a necessity. The once "prosperous," childless couple who earned $80,000 now barely made ends meet, using 80 percent of their income to pay their mortgage and two car payments. Why didn't the bank tell them this could happen?

When you apply for a mortgage, the people who process your application are concerned with only your *present* paycheck. They don't anticipate your future. They don't factor in that you may need a new car or that you may have additional children.

> *The only thing constant about life is change, and relying on your present circumstances can have disastrous effects when qualifying for a mortgage.*

On the other hand, it is also possible that Jack's income can double or triple as he improves in his profession, which would be phenomenal. But one must consider all *projected* expenses with a substantial raise, plus the costs of raising a family.

The cost of raising children is amazing. It has been estimated that the cost of raising a child until he or she is 17 can range from $151,170 to $293,400, depending upon whether you qualify as a low-income family (earning under $29,000 per year) or a high income family (earning over $48,300 per year).[1]

To plan for your home, you should rely on only one

breadwinner's income to make sure you qualify for the mortgage, and your mortgage payment should be absolutely no more than 20 percent of your weekly take-home pay.

Qualify Yourself to Avoid Disaster

Most people never truly do a thorough budget analysis. They are taken with the prospect of purchasing a home. They assume that, if they qualify, everything is fine. Remember that over one million people filed for bankruptcy from July 1, 2001, to June 30, 2002[2], and among them, those who owned their homes initially "qualified" for their mortgage.

I see people whose mortgage payments constitute over 75 percent of their take-home pay. How can they possibly avoid debt when they don't have enough money to pay for necessities?

Before you purchase any home, you should keep track of your expenses for one full year.

If you have never lived in a house before, you cannot anticipate how much home maintenance and utilities will cost. Many expenses can be controlled by simplification, but if you're caught up in keeping up with the Jones, you will pay for landscapers, several home improvements, pools, cleaning services and other expenses that could be avoided. Check with future neighbors or the utility companies regarding how much your normal monthly obligation would be. You must be aware of your regular expenses; if you don't properly anticipate them, you will be debt ridden.

Remember, even though you get a tax deduction for a mortgage payment, you still have to be able to pay it. What good is a major tax deduction if you can't meet the monthly obligation?

One expense that can clearly be within your control is the phone. It is amazing how much people can run up their phone bill. Also, cable TV is another expense that can be controlled. Some people who have incurred thousands of dollars in credit card debts spend over $100 per month for cable TV.

What about maintenance and repairs? How do you anticipate those expenses? If you buy a handyman's special, you can expect to spend regularly for repairs. Even if you have had a thorough inspection of a home, all homes eventually need work. If you are fortunate enough to be able to do repair and maintenance work yourself, you must still consider the cost of supplies and equipment.

One problem I've seen is when people use every penny for their deposit and closing costs and then have no leftover funds for home emergencies. Eventually, you are going to need repairs for roofs, heating, air conditioning, plumbing, plus a host of other contingencies that you have to anticipate.

How do you prepare for home maintenance? You put away a few thousand dollars for an emergency.

Get a Grip on the Necessities

Every family has to eat, and you should have a good idea how much you spend on food. The cost of food is tied in with the size of your family. If you purchase a home while childless and suddenly have three children over the course of your home ownership, the cost of your monthly food expenses will substantially increase. Also, once the children become teenagers, the food bill will be even larger. A major problem for many clients I've met over the years is that they have no idea how much they spend on food. It is true that you can use coupons and go to special clubs or discount stores; however, I have a hard time comprehending how a family of four can realistically have a grocery bill of less than $300 per month.

Let's assume that you live moderately. You can control certain expenses for food if you buy bulk or use coupons. However, even if you brown bag and don't eat out all the time, you have to anticipate groceries, for a two-person household, at a minimum of $300 per month, and it would be a lot higher if you eat out or buy a lot of processed foods. Please note that if you have any additional children, food expenses will go up substantially. It has always been my experience that you can't skimp on food. However, think about your eating habits. Do you stop in you local convenience store every day and get your coffee and pastry? This could cost an extra $50 a month — just for breakfast. Do you brown bag your lunch or order out everyday? People who order out every day can spend an additional $100 per month. Finally, eating out for dinner can substantially raise your food budget.

Before you even think about a mortgage, I want you to get a notebook and actually write out what you spend on necessities, such as food.

How much do you spend at the grocery store each month? Make sure you consider paper products, diapers, "special" foods and anything else. Also, consider the size of your family; if you have one or two children and plan to have additional kids, no matter how frugal you are, the food budget is going to go up. This is the case regardless of the fact that you use coupons or go to the discount food store. People have to eat.

Clothing is another necessity that we all need. I am not talking about designer clothing, although that is a realistic expense for certain families. In larger families, children can wear hand-me-downs. However, if clothes are torn or shoes are without soles, it is necessary to purchase new clothes.

Again, if you have teenagers, who never seem to stop growing and eating, you will have to allocate more money for clothing. It is not always easy to anticipate your clothing budget if your family is growing. However, use a budget of the past year's clothing budget to give you a start. Unfortunately, many people I come into contact with don't realize how much they spend on clothing, since they just run it up on their credit cards.

Besides a larger family, do you have a job that requires you to purchase work clothing, or do you have to dress the part? You may spend a substantial amount on clothing under these circumstances. If you spend a few hundred dollars per month on clothing, and don't have enough money to make ends meet, you need to be very careful about what type of mortgage commitment you get.

Before you consider expenses, you have to anticipate utilities, which are a crucial part of your budget. It is extremely difficult to anticipate certain utilities based on the size of the home. However, if you simplify, you can eliminate certain unnecessary costs such as cable TV, satellite TV and large electric, gas and phone bills that are not necessary.

Another expense is payment of association fees, if you purchase a townhouse, and condo association fees, if you purchase a condominium. Please note that these expenses are also subject to change based on the whims of an association. Thus, before you get locked into a condominium or townhouse, be aware of these expenses.

Finally, home maintenance, car repairs and medical expenses cannot be anticipated with a certainty, but they have to be made part of the planning process before you commit yourself to a mortgage.

This is a very monumental decision. Before you commit yourself to it, plan out all the contingencies so that you won't find yourself in debt.

Another expense, which is often overlooked, is laundry and dry cleaning. If you have a washing machine at home, that expense will usually be incorporated into electric and gas. However, some occupations require dry cleaning on a regular basis, and it could easily run over $100 per month. People frequently fail to contemplate all these monthly expenses before they purchase a home.

Medical expenses are crucial, and most young couples who purchase their first home do not even contemplate any type of medical emergency. Unfortunately, this is something that is difficult to anticipate. The only thing that I can advise you, which will be discussed in more depth later, is to protect yourself with insurance. I am not a physician, but you can certainly help maintain health if you eat right, exercise moderately, eliminate toxins from your life, and try to avoid stress.

One way to avoid stress is to have your finances under control.

Again, as with repairs, I would try to establish some type of nest egg to protect against normal expenses for doctors, dentists and prescriptions that are not covered by insurance.

Consider Your Car

Another important budgeting item is transportation. First, you have to consider whether you have a car payment. As I will explain later, car payments and especially leases, are not recommended, since there can be substantial ramifications that create debt. It is important to understand this perspective if you must finance a vehicle. Remember that a vehicle doesn't make you sexier, younger, faster or cooler . . . it is only a means of transportation.

You want to have a reliable car that will last and not be a financial drain to operate.

In considering the costs of transportation, the initial cost will be gasoline. In 1979, at the height of the energy crisis and long lines at the gas pumps, mileage per gallon was a major advertising scheme. However, fuel economy doesn't seem to be a major selling point any longer; but, with gasoline prices continually escalating, it is always subject to change. The key issue is safety, which it should be. However, fuel economy shouldn't be totally disregarded since there is a big difference between the cost of maintaining and repairing a luxury vehicle and an economy vehicle. Naturally, the overall costs of owning a Mercedes will be substantially higher that a Ford Escort. You will pay more for gasoline, parts, maintenance and insurance. However, with continuing increases in gas prices and an economy that relies more and more on foreign oil supplies, gasoline prices should not be disregarded. If you need an SUV for your family, you have every right as an American to have that vehicle. Just remember that the SUV will be a lot more expensive to run than will the economy vehicle. Be aware, too, that many economy vehicles are getting 50 miles per gallon and more, due to new technologies.

We live in a free country in which you can have any material object you desire. But a car is your second largest investment. If you spend too much on the vehicle, it may reduce your opportunity to purchase the right home. Even if the Mercedes is paid in full, you have to factor in the costs tied with owning and operating the more expensive vehicle.

Add Up the Little things

Have you ever really analyzed and written down how much you spend a year on recreation, clubs, entertainment, newspapers and magazines? It is amazing how minor variations in these expenses can save hundreds of dollars per month. The reason I suggest you figure out *yearly* expenses is that you want to calculate how much you spend on holidays, birthdays, parties and activities for your kids — expenses that aren't reflected in monthly expenses. You would be amazed how many people don't want to deprive their kids of Christmas gifts but, in the process of making their children happy, will let their mortgage fall behind.

Poor financial choices can deprive a family of their home, neighborhood, school and friends.

However, even a budget analysis is not going to be 100 percent accurate. One year you may experience minimal "emergency" expenses, while the next year you may have $4,000 in home maintenance, $3,000 in car repairs, and develop a medical condition that also incurs more expenses.

For readers who have children, do you know how much you spend a month on gifts for parties, entertainment or just snacks?

I have said that many people living on fixed paychecks spend $5.00 *every* morning on breakfast and coffee at the local convenience store and $5.00 *every* day on lunch. These are not self-employed persons who have certain tax write-offs. If you add in another $25.00 per week spent on cigarettes, they spend over $300.00 per month on items that are clearly not necessities. This doesn't even count eating out, shows, games and vacations. Recreation is very necessary, since constant work will eventually have negative implications on your health. However, unless you are truly financially independent or are single with no responsibility, the $300 per month expenses are totally out of control. They could be used to prepay your mortgage or car loan or to put money away into investments. If you plan to allocate $2,000 for a vacation, you could save that money by cutting back on the aforementioned expenses for seven months.

Charitable contributions are important, since people have to learn to give to receive, and there are several wonderful charities. The only thing that I caution you to learn — before you give — is the percentage of your contribution that actually goes to the charity. Are you really giving to the charity, or are you helping to pay John Doe's $80,000-per-year salary as administrator? Several clients of mine tithe their income. I think it is truly wonderful if you tithe your income to your church or synagogue. But, again, if you barely can afford necessities and tithe your income at the expense of your other bills, then you have to rethink your priorities.

Insure a Financially Fit Future

A major expense that most people don't anticipate is cost of insurance. To avoid major medical problems, and the horrendous bills they can create, you must have health insurance. This could run anywhere from $150 per month for a single person to over $700 per family. These rates can change substantially, depending on what company you use. This is another factor that can substantially cut down on your take-home pay. When this book was written, health insurance costs were continuing to escalate.

In addition to the expenses for medical insurance, you also have to include life insurance, if you have a family, and disability insurance, if you are self-employed.

Insurance doesn't create wealth, but it is totally necessary to protect you from financial disaster.

For example, if you don't have automobile insurance, besides facing civil and quasi-criminal penalties, you can face financial consequences and lose everything you own. Further, liability insurance is necessary for any business, and homeowners insurance is necessary to protect you from burglary, fire and several other types of unforeseen problems. You should know what insurance is necessary, and the costs involved, otherwise you will be on the road to debt and may lose everything you've worked for.

Does your mortgage *include* taxes and insurance, or are you responsible for taxes and homeowners insurance? Most people feel it is easier to have the mortgage company be responsible for everything. I don't. If your mortgage company is responsible for these costs, they can put forced-place insurance on the property, which can cost substantially more than if you get insurance yourself. However, you will pay a price for letting them handle taxes and insurance. If real estate taxes go up, you can budget the increase over the year; but if your mortgage company has to absorb this increase, the escrow adjustment may be substantially higher than the tax increase. It is much better to take responsibility and set aside money for real estate taxes. The alternative is that your mortgage company could escrow the funds, and your mortgage payment could drastically change. And you certainly don't want to finance the cost of insurance or taxes over the life of the mortgage.

You should try to create as much stability as possible with your mortgage payments, since so many other monthly expenses are unpredictable.

I will repeat that, to maintain a life without debt in a world full of change, you should try to have as much certainty as possible.

Scheduled Expenses Must Be Considered

Do you have substantial amount of installment payments on consumer items? This is a very dangerous situation you are in, because these expenses are added to all your necessities and the unexpected expenses.

A sure sign that you are in debt is your having to make monthly installment payments.

Another major expense, which most people fail to consider in their budgeting, is gifts and expenses for parties, weddings, bar mitzvahs and other celebrations. Life-cycle events are very important, but people should never mortgage their homes or take a loan to pay for such events. Some people are so concerned with impressing friends and family members that they lose all perspective about what they spend for parties and celebrations.

So many of my clients got into debt by spending substantial

sums of money for Christmas, and they never calculated that into their budget. There is absolutely nothing wrong if you spend a large sum for family and friends, but not at the expense of your mortgage. You must consider these expenses in analyzing your initial budget to see how much of a mortgage you can afford.

You also have to anticipate the normal expenses for children, which can include sports activities, lessons, dance schools, parties and other incidental expenses. As evidenced from statistics, costs of raising children is substantial, and most of my clients have failed to budget for the dollar here and there — the class trips, the uniforms and any other miscellaneous expenses tied to children. This is why, if you don't consider a growing family, there could be substantial additional expenses later.

One Can — and Should — Do It

Let's say the basis for your qualification was the paychecks of both you and your spouse. As with Jack and Jill, they were both earning substantial salaries. But two years later, with the birth of their child, they had to incur full-time daycare for Jill to keep her job. This is a major, unanticipated expense that people never think to include. People have to not only know their budget, when they are looking to purchase a home, they have to anticipate the costs of children, balance whether both spouses should work, and consider the resulting costs if one spouse does work.

You should never rely on both spouses' incomes when determining what type of mortgage is best for you.

Why don't I suggest that you use two spouse's incomes to qualify for a mortgage? First let's assume the female breadwinner has to go on maternity leave. If you rely on both salaries to meet all of your bills, the leave may cause an extreme drop in income. Also, if children come into the picture, as I have said, you may have to consider substantial childcare expenses, which offset the income even if both spouses are employed.

The second reason for you to rely on only one spouse's income is that it is much more important that one spouse use his or her salary for savings. The only way to avoid being set up for financial problems is to have one spouse's income pay the expenses while the other spouse saves and eventually works on investments. This will force two-income families to develop discipline and learn to live within their means rather than letting their wants get them into debt.

If you are single and want to purchase a home, you can still follow the formula, because a condo or townhouse is usually much less expensive. Further, a condo or townhouse may be a starter home, so you want to have the flexibility of being able to purchase a larger home when you start a family.

Another practical reason to count the earnings of only one spouse is that the only constant in life is change. If you rely on both breadwinners, what will you do in case of an accident, disability, illness, loss of job, or maternity? Life changes can alter the initial budget that you came up with when you decided to purchase a home years ago. If one spouse had used his or her income solely for savings and investments, it would have become an automatic safety net, and the couple could temporarily switch from saving to paying the household bills. Any leftover amounts could then be saved.

Consider the Cost of Property

You should never get an adjustable-rate mortgage. Others would disagree with me, stating that if you are not planning to live in the home for more that a few years, the numbers can work in your favor. However, the key to living a life without debt is to have a regular mortgage payment that will not alter and that you can pay off quicker than 30 years or 15 years, depending on your mortgage. If you take a $100,000 30-year mortgage at 7 percent, with payments of $665.30 per month, you will be paying back $239,508.90 over 30 years.

If you prepay your mortgage by only $100 extra per month, you will pay the mortgage company only $189,001.74 and save $50,507.16 by prepaying principal.[3] This is why the second spouse's income should be used for investment or prepayment of the mortgage.

Another folk tale I frequently hear is that, to cut taxes, you should have a large mortgage because you will get a tax deduction. However, incurring debt is a very dangerous proposition, because it does not build net worth. Also, if your circumstances change, as in the case of Jack and Jill, you are stuck with a substantial debt load. I have seen too many people get tied up in investment properties who are now tied up with bankruptcies — all because their income changed. They can't rent out the properties or just aren't receiving the rent, which they rely upon to pay the mortgage.

Even assuming you only have one property, if you don't have the income to afford the mortgage, the tax deduction won't mean a damned thing, since tax deductions are only useful when you have the income.

It does no good to have a tax deduction if you have no income to support it.

Manage the Mortgage

To follow my rule that the mortgage payment should equal 20 percent or less of the breadwinner's net monthly pay, you are going to have to save a substantial amount of money to buy a home. Based on the one-breadwinner theory, the second breadwinner's income can be used to prepay principal.

If you purchased a home with a $60,000 mortgage over 30

years, and the mortgage payment is $451 for 30 years, you would end up paying the mortgage company $162,360 over 30 years.

However, how the $451 is *applied* the first few years and the last years of the mortgage payment, differs dramatically. If you checked an amortization table, the initial payments are applied toward interest the first few years. Subsequently, as you pay more of the mortgage payments over the 30 years, more of the mortgage payment will be applied toward principal, based on the amortization table. A way to save substantial interest is to send a separate check, labeled "Payment on Principal," to the mortgage company. This will go right to principal toward your goal of satisfying the mortgage.

Be extremely cautious about refinancing your mortgage. Understand all costs involved. Try to find a mortgage company that won't assign its interest. I have seen disastrous circumstances in which people who thought they were dealing with "A" mortgage company. Two years later "A" assigned its interest to "B", "B" assigned its interest to "C", and "C" assigned its interest to "D".

As previously discussed, stability with your mortgage is very important for financial security. When you're dealing with the same mortgage company for years, you are hoping for some type of personal relationship. (I don't know how possible this is with banks constantly buying out each other.)

However, the biggest pitfall occurs when "A" mortgage assigns its interest to "B" mortgage, and "B" mortgage may misplace records due to computer glitches. This can result in false allegations that you are behind on mortgage payments, and you will have the burden of showing all past receipts to prevent foreclosure.

I recently had a client who got a letter from her mortgage company stating that she was $50,000 behind in her mortgage payments. This was a case where the original mortgage was assigned to another mortgage company. After extensive analysis, the mortgage company found it had made a substantial mistake in not crediting my client with thousands of dollars in mortgage payments.

Remember, under the law you also have to be able to produce receipts or you are presumed to be in default. Beware of fly-by-night mortgage companies that assign their interest to other companies.

Pay your mortgage before any other debts.

Remember to get a home with a mortgage payment that is within your means. You are the one who is contractually obligated to pay that mortgage, not the eager mortgage broker or real estate broker. If the bank's assessments of who "qualifies" were always correct, then nobody would ever lose their home in a foreclosure.

You have to use your common sense when you get approved for a mortgage. If, when you look at your yearly income and expenses, the potential mortgage payment constitute 50 percent of your net monthly income, it should raise a big red flag. You know that, with all the other expenses, it just won't work. If a second mortgage raises that ratio, then you have to really wonder.

If you don't plan for emergencies then emergencies will find you.

Finally

Even though there is no tax benefit or equity in renting, it is a short-term endeavor that can help you save for a home. It is beneficial for you to sacrifice and save before you commit to a home. You must work out the numbers. Follow the 20 percent rule, or you will open yourself to a life of scarcity rather than abundance. We all want a nice home in a nice neighborhood with quality schools; however, make sure you're comfortable with the numbers, and make sure you can sustain the payments before you sign on the dotted line.

Buying a home is the biggest investment you will ever have. If you *mis*anticipate, it can have incredible consequences on all aspects of your life. You have worked too hard to end up losing it all. Use your common sense. You can always buy "up" later, when you develop the equity.

Do your homework, and it will keep you free from debt.

Monthly Expenditures Checklist

_____ Mortgage/Rent
_____ Electric
_____ Gas
_____ Oil
_____ Kerosene
_____ Water
_____ Sewage
_____ Cable
_____ Telephone
_____ Cell Phone
_____ Home Repairs & Maintenance
_____ Groceries, including paper products
_____ Clothing
_____ Laundry & Dry cleaning
_____ Medical Co-payments, Prescriptions & Dental Expenses
_____ Gasoline
_____ Tolls
_____ Transportation
_____ Recreation, Eating Out
_____ Vacations
_____ Gifts for Birthdays & Holidays
_____ Charitable Contributions
_____ Insurance

_____ Homeowners
_____ Life
_____ Health
_____ Auto
_____ Disability
_____ Other
_____ Real Estate Taxes
_____ Auto payments
_____ Furniture Payments
_____ Timeshare
_____ Appliance Payments
_____ Credit card Payments
_____ Student loans
_____ Child Support
_____ Alimony
_____ Daycare
_____ Baby-sitter
_____ Car repairs
_____ Cigarettes
_____ Haircuts
_____ Clubs
_____ Newspapers
_____ Magazines
_____ Other _______________
_____ Other _______________
_____ Other _______________
_____ Other _______________
_____ Other _______________
_____ Other _______________
_____ Other _______________

Chapter 2

Choosing Your Partner

Another major reason that people find themselves in financial difficulties is that they choose the wrong partners. A broken relationship after a child arrives can cost the obligor child support payments for years, which creates a never-ending financial burden. Women who end up obtaining custody of children from a broken relationship are on the other side of the financial mess. Some single moms chose irresponsible men who fail to pay support. Even the luckier ones, who do get support, lose financially.

Even when people have had children out of the current marriage relationship, a breakdown in the marriage results in divorce, which creates unbearable emotional heartache plus financial loss for both parties. Income that used to cover one family is then required to pay for two households. Debt is incurred with child support, spousal support, and extremely costly legal fees. Only the lawyers win.

Too many people are looking for instant gratification and won't work on the marriage when things get tough. Marriage is a very special institution that is not only between two people — it is also blessed by God. It is a holy covenant.

Marriage is like the highway of life. You have periods of easy, straight roads, but other periods can get extremely bumpy. When you get married, this should be taken very seriously, since marriage is not a situation that you can just leave. The marriage covenant is for sickness and health until death do you part. Unfortunately, in our age of instantaneous gratification, people give up immediately if their spouse goes through hard times — financially, emotionally, or spiritually — rather than realizing that they are "one". With all the media's fixation on youth and beauty, there will come a time where anyone can always find a spouse who is younger, richer or more attractive. However, divorce should be the exception only in extreme cases.

The High Cost of Divorce

The result of divorce is usually a financial disaster, especially when children are involved. In addition, the stress and emotional baggage create additional costs for doctors and therapists. I have trouble understanding how people, who have been so intimate through the marriage relationship, can suddenly destroys this covenant, which results in unbearable consequences.

Besides the emotional aspects of breakup and divorce, studies have shown that single women are statistically more inclined to suffer financially. In a recent study by Oliver B. Pollak of the Commercial Law League of America, he analyzed consumer bankruptcy filings in the state of Nebraska for 1977, 1987 and 1997. From 1977 to 1997 the percentage of women, individually filing bankruptcy had tripled.[1] It is true that the *total* number of bankruptcies for men and married couples had also increased but women filing individually had tripled.

According to research by Professors Teresa Sullivan and Elizabeth Warren, women filing bankruptcy alone in the first quarter of 1999 made up 39 percent of all filers, outnumbering single filing men and married couples.[2] In 1981, single filing women constituted 17 percent of all filers, while in 1991, single filing women constituted 30 percent of all filers.[3] Furthermore, from January 1997 through June 1999, 14,644 Nebraska residents filed bankruptcy, of which 34 percent were individual women.[4] These studies don't specify whether the individual women were single, married, single with children, or divorced; however, it is evident that more women are filing bankruptcy. One reason is that 300,000 single female debtors are owed child support.[5]

Why are women in such abysmal debt that they have to get to a point of filing bankruptcy? One reason is that the divorce population is the fastest growing category of the population, and that is one of the major factors that puts women on the welfare lines. Studies show that, in most cases, a divorced woman is not as economically well off as when she was married. Also, the woman is still more likely to be awarded custody of the children. Even though women usually get child support, it does still not prevent poverty, in many cases. Studies also show that in 1996 families with female households, no husband present, showed 35.8 percent of all families in this category were below the poverty level.[6]

Defining Today's American Family

Another area to understand is the breakdown of the traditional American family. First you have to understand how the Census Bureau defines an American Household. An individual in the household is designated as the householder (the person who owns or rents the house). Households are further divided into family households and non-family household in that it contains at least one relative of the householder, while a non-family household consists of a person living alone or living only with nonrelatives. Thereafter, family households are divided into families maintained by married couples and "other families" maintained by men or women with no spouse at home. The Bureau of Census treats a family household as a group of two or more people sharing a home, related by birth, marriage or adoption. Therefore, a single parent with children or siblings sharing a house or any combinations of relatives with no spouse are considered family households.[7]

Since 1940 the percentage of family households has decreased from 90 percent to 69.5 percent in 1997.[8] Further, from 1975 to 1996, the percentage of married women (with children) in the work force has increased from 44.9 percent to 71.1 percent.[9] The relationship between the decline of family households and the increase of working mothers shows a major shift in the American family.

A Family's Worth

Why did more people file bankruptcy during the nineties than ever before? One clue is evident if you examine the income for different types of families. You will see the following breakdown: In 1996, married-couple families earned an average of $61,345, while male householders with no wife earned $43,751, and female householders with no husband earned $28,348. When you examine the statistics, a female householder living alone is at the bottom of the rung at $21,874.[10] Thus, the single woman is statistically at the lowest financial level compared to male and family households.

Since 1966, the American family has also changed in the percentage of families that are married-couple families. Father-only and mother-only families with minor children have shifted dramatically since 1966. In 1966, only 2,728 thousand families were "single" parent families, while 24,276 thousand married-couple families existed with minor children. In 1997, the "single" parent families increased to 9,583 thousand families, while married-couple families increased to only 25,083 thousand.[11]

The Influence of Social Assistance

With the increase in debt and bankruptcies also came the massive increase in Social Security and social welfare spending. The whole notion of Social Security arose from the Great Depression. However, in 1940, only 222,000 people received Social Security benefits, while in 1998 over 44,000,000 people received Social Security checks. In addition, SSI's inception was in 1974 and 3,249,000 people received benefits, while in 1998, 6,566,000 people obtained SSI. The outpouring of federal funding for Social Security has grown from 1,278,000 in 1937 to 26,675,000,000 in 1997.[12]

Social welfare, in general, has increased from 24,956.6 million in 1960 to 852,621.9 million in 1994.[13] In 1950, social welfare expenditures totaled 8.8 percent of the gross domestic product, while in 1994 social welfare expenditures constituted 21.0 percent of gross domestic product.[14] Since 1985, social welfare expenditures have constituted about 50 percent of all federal spending; however, these expenditures have been rising as a percentage of state and local government costs from 69 percent in 1985 to 74 percent in 1994.[15]

Even with the alleged booming economy during the Clinton administration, the demand for welfare assistance, with few exceptions, has increased sharply over the past several years. Again, the households that were more likely to receive means-tested assistance were single, female-headed families. It is clearly evident that when a female has children outside of marriage or has a marriage which terminates in divorce, according to all the government statistics, she has the greatest chance of being debt ridden in need of some type of government assistance. There is a direct correlation between the increase of women with children considered in need of government assistance and the Nebraska model, which shows that bankruptcies for females have tripled in the past 29 years.

A Reason to Be Picky

By failing to plan what type of men they associate with or marry, women are immediately setting themselves up for financial disaster, because many are still on the poverty line if they are receiving child support or if they have to live off credit cards to pay the rent, mortgage or buy their children food and shelter. Thus, the notion of out-of-wedlock pregnancy can have many more far-reaching consequences, aside from the fact that it forces many young girls to drop out of school. The bottom line is that sex with the wrong person, whether married or unmarried, generates financial problems. A good marriage does not guarantee that you won't get in debt; however, a strong, loving family in which both parties help each other is less likely to start out with two strikes before they even get up to bat.

These are very complex issues, and almost everyone has made mistakes in choosing relationships. Unfortunately, it comes down to the procreation question. If you date somebody and you realize that you are not right for each other, you just move on and find the next person. The problem results when children arrive. Once childbearing enters the picture, serious consequences occur. If your partner lacks character, there will be substantial social, emotional, and economic consequences.

Children need both parents to have a secure upbringing. However, without getting into the psychological problems, let's look at the financial consequences. Single women with kids get hit the hardest.

On the other hand, men who make wrong choices may be stuck with child support obligations that drain their paychecks for years, creating long-term indebtedness.

Choosing the wrong partner can dramatically influence your financial future.

What to Look for In a Partner

Choosing the right partner can affect your financial situation for years to come. Anytime you enter into a committed relationship or marriage, there is a risk. However, certain behaviors can raise red flags:

Loyalty — Is he/she the type who makes a commitment, or is he/she the life-of-the-party-type who will move on when something better comes along?

Selfishness — Is he/she focused on only individual likes and dislikes? Is compromise a possibility? Be careful when someone is obsessed with himself/herself.

Spending Habits — Is he/she into conspicuous consumption? Are image and status key rather than sincerity and commitment? Are credit cards used indiscriminately when cash isn't available?

Debt — Is he/she overwhelmed with credit card debt, student loans and car payments? Is there honesty about the debt and a plan for recovery?

Morality — Is he/she moral and committed, regardless of challenges? Is there sensitivity or disdain toward others with problems?

Sacrifice — Is he/she interested in only you? Do you have a caring partner who gives time to a friend, relative or charity with needs?

Jealousy — If there is jealousy, it could destroy trust, which in turn destroys a relationship.

Trust — Without total trust in your partner, a relationship cannot work.

Religious Views — Arguments over religion are extremely dangerous to a relationship. Having similar religious views helps bolster a relationship.

Political Views — Are both of you similar in your political views? When two people have similar belief systems, it is less likely that rifts will occur in the relationship.

Economic Views — Are both parties on the same page economically? Do you view money, spending and debt on the same wavelength? Since financial issues are key to any relationship, major differences in this area can cause problems.

Lifestyle — Do you have similar lifestyles? Is one partner constantly traveling while the other is more settled?

Family — Do your families get along? Are they local or is family out of the area? How dependent is one partner to his/her family?

Temperament — Are both parties calm or high strung? Does one person have a bad temper? Are you both accepting and forgiving?

Stability — Are both parties stable with their employment and relationships? Has one partner constantly switched jobs while the other has stability in his/her job? Is one party always seeking change while the other party is set in his/her lifestyle?

Since the breakdown in a relationship can cause serious financial implications when children are involved, it is crucial to try to make the right choice in your commitments.

I am not a psychologist, but I have met thousands of people during my lifetime. To make any relationship successful, you have to work at it. However, if you start off with several red flags, it could lead to problems that can result in financial disaster.

Chapter 3

Baby, You Can Drive My Car

Unless you live in an urban area, most suburban areas make it difficult to commute without a motor vehicle. Where public transportation exists, you probably still need a vehicle to get to a speed line or metro station. In some rural areas, public transportation just doesn't exist at all. If you aren't situated in a major metropolitan area or work in the city, you are going to need private transportation.

Next to your home, your vehicle is going to be the next largest investment you will make. The bottom line is that, without transportation, you severely limit your employment opportunities, so you need reliable transportation. However, the media continues to perpetuate the myth that you need a new, loaded vehicle. Even though a motor vehicle is merely a means of transportation to get you from point A to point B, many people feel the need to enhance their image through the vehicle they drive.

The problem arises when you finance or lease a vehicle and pay astronomical amounts in interest and insurance when the bank has a lien on your vehicle.

Why is there such a desire for new vehicles? If you watch TV, listen to the radio, read magazines, newspapers or any other media, cars are always advertised. However, the car companies are not selling cars, they are selling sex, freedom, status, prestige and anything else Madison Avenue dictates. Furthermore, banks are actively soliciting high-risk customers. They advertise "Bad Credit, No Credit, No Problem", and they even accept bankruptcies. "No Money Down, No Payments for Three Months, Low Financing." So many people want a vehicle that they don't even know the interest rate as long as the payment seems right. Many consumers don't read and don't realize that they are still responsible for payments regardless of repairs, huge insurance premiums or other hidden expenses that go with financing.

There is a constant fear that if someone has an older vehicle, it is not reliable. Thus, many of my clients tie themselves to financing ridiculous amounts without even knowing the interest rate. What's even more amazing is that people pay such huge payments on lease payments where they acquire no equity. It is incredible that people sign valid financing agreements without even knowing the interest rate they are paying on the vehicle. Further, they don't realize the astronomical amount they pay for car insurance, because you need complete collision and comprehensive coverage when a bank is a lienholder.

Do You Really Need a New Car?

Is it really necessary to have a new vehicle? There are several quality vehicles that can be purchased for low amounts of money without incurring ridiculous payments and substantial insurance increases. There is absolutely no tax benefit for interest payments that are made on car payments. People forget that motor vehicles depreciate incredibly. If you are financing a vehicle and there is an accident or it is stolen, you may be responsible for any deficiency after the insurance company pays the bank, unless you carry gap insurance. Even assuming that a used vehicle will require a certain amount of repairs and maintenance, the savings on no car payments and lower insurance rates will make up for any upkeep.

Just because you are financing a new vehicle, the warranty is still *limited* and doesn't guarantee that you won't have maintenance and repair costs. Most of these warranties are for three years or 36,000 miles, and people who commute a lot have no protection once they pass those limits. If you get an extended warranty, for a used vehicle, please read the small print to see what benefits you are truly receiving.

If you want to avoid debt, you should purchase a good, reliable, used vehicle. Then you can save the monthly expense you would have paid for financing and eventually pay cash for a new vehicle.

However, never finance a used vehicle, because you don't know whose problems you are inheriting. I see people who pay astronomical payments for six-year-old vehicles. These cars have no warranty and will incur the same repairs as the used vehicles you could have paid cash for. However, before you purchase a used vehicle, have a reliable mechanic do a thorough examination. If the vehicle has been properly maintained, it should be just as reliable as a new vehicle.

In 1990, we purchased a 7-year-old vehicle with over 100,000 miles. The car needed some work, but it lasted very well for over three years until the cost of the transmission was more than the vehicle was worth. My point is that it is better to have a reliable vehicle and save for another "new" vehicle than to tie yourself into a financing arrangement that can hurt you financially or destroy your credit.

A Lesson on Leases

Be especially careful of the "No Money Down" ads. These ads are usually for leases. Leases sound very attractive, since there may be no money down and minimal payments. However, unless you are a business, there is no benefit to lease and you build no equity. You may be paying $400 per month for four years and have zero equity after paying for four years. After the lease expires, you will have to pay the residual value of the vehicle if you want to buy it. Also, if you return the vehicle, you may be responsible for mileage if you go over 12,000 miles per year, and you may have to pay for any excessive wear and tear. Thus, after the illusion of no money or limited money down, you have no equity, large insurance payments, plus a large monthly payment due to the finance company.

A Lesson on Loans

If you decide to finance a vehicle, make sure you understand all costs associated with the loan. Understand the interest rate, know the NADA or blue book values, and see if the dealer is throwing in unnecessary options to boost the cost of the vehicle. Be wary of paying for any "additional" benefits such as warranties, insurance, disability insurance, and other add-ons that skyrocket the cost of the vehicle. Compare dealers to get the best price.

Timing is also very important. Don't look for a car on a sunny day. The best time to shop is when dealers are unloading prior-year models to make room for the new vehicles, the end of the year for tax benefits for the dealer, or when there is bad weather. How many people want to shop for a new car when the weather is lousy? You can usually get a good bargain since you will be one of the few customers in the shop. Another benefit is that you can test the safety of the vehicle and see how it handles in poor weather conditions.

Once you get in the finance game, you are being controlled by the payment rather than the quality of the vehicle. I have seen people who don't worry about the quality, cost, interest rate or any other facts, as long as they can afford the payment. The car may be worth $7,000, and you are paying $300 per month for five years, but you have a "payment" that fits your budget. Thus, the cost of purchasing the vehicle is irrelevant if the monthly payment is affordable. Remember, all the gimmicks about "No Money Down, No Payments Until After Christmas" are there to sucker you in. Car dealers are not in business to give you free things; they are there to make a profit. They make this profit by not selling a vehicle but selling a "feeling" at a price you can afford.

The biggest problem with purchasing a vehicle that is financed is as follows:

1. The costs of financing have no tax benefits, and the interest rates are always higher than what you will earn on investments. If I am wrong and you can get a lower interest rate than you are earning on your investment, then go ahead and finance.

2. When you finance a vehicle, your auto insurance goes up substantially, because you have to pay for complete comprehensive and collision insurance and list the bank as loss payee. Also, you must have lower deductibles, which substantially raise the costs of auto insurance.

3. How many consumers know the interest rate before they finance a vehicle? How many people know the added cost of credit life insurance, warranties, and other costs that are incorporated into the payment? How many people look at the NADA or Blue Book before they purchase a vehicle?

4. Financing complicates matters. Between all the costs for additional auto insurance premiums, down payments, warranties, credit life and interest, you could have purchased a reliable, used vehicle. (If you got a no-money-down variety, you are probably paying even more outrageous costs). If you start cutting out certain unnecessary items in your budget, you would then have some money available to save for purchasing a reliable vehicle. How many people buy a vehicle because it runs well? How many buy a vehicle because it is sporty, fast, powerful or prestigious? People will allege they must have minivans, since they have large families. How did families manage before minivans? They used station wagons.

If All Else Fails, Finance

If you must finance because you have absolutely no cash available, finance for as short a period as possible, since the longer you finance, the larger the interest payment to the bank. There are several ways that financing a vehicle can substantially increase your potential for debt. When you finance a vehicle, you must remember that vehicles depreciate substantially. Let's say you purchase a vehicle for $15,000 and pay $300 per month for a five-year note. However, five years later you are paying the same amount for a vehicle that is worth substantially less than when you purchased it. In addition, when you finance a vehicle after the warranty is over, you will be responsible for repairs. Most warranties are for three years or 36,000 miles, so if you drive a lot, the warranty will be over quickly. Regardless of maintenance and repairs, you will still have the monthly obligation. In addition, you still have the added insurance premium when you are financing a vehicle. You need low deductibles, complete coverage, plus you must list the finance company as loss payee.

How Financing Can Ruin Your Credit

Financing can seriously damage your credit when certain events occur that are outside of your control:

1. *Repossession or voluntary repossession.* Let's say you are approved for an auto loan and suddenly your company is downsized. If you financed a relatively new vehicle or leased a similar vehicle, and fall behind on payments, the car will be repossessed. (If you realized you could no longer afford the vehicle, there would be a voluntary surrender). Once either the repossession or voluntary repossession occurs, your credit is severely damaged, plus you will usually owe money after the vehicle is sold.

2. *Theft.* If you are financing a vehicle that is worth less than you owe, you will be responsible to the bank the difference in what is owed and what the insurance paid, unless you carry gap insurance — an additional cost. Thus, due to no fault of you own, you can owe a substantial amount of money on a financed vehicle that has been stolen.

3. *Accident.* The same thing applies to a vehicle that is involved in an accident and totaled. If a drunk smashes into you and totals your new vehicle, the insurance company will pay the value of the vehicle, and you owe a substantial debt on this vehicle. The only way to avoid this situation is to incur the additional cost of gap insurance.

4. *Depreciation.* Cars and trucks depreciate substantially. You purchase a car in 1999 for $15,000 and pay $300 per month for a five-year note. However, in four years you are still paying the same amount for a vehicle that has substantially less value than when you purchased it. So by the time you get done paying for a $15,000 vehicle, you are paying the same $300

payment for a vehicle that has depreciated substantially.

5. *Repairs.* No matter how well you maintain your vehicle, there are going to eventually be breakdowns, which will require substantial costs. Most importantly, you will still have to maintain that monthly payment and high car insurance payment, regardless of the cost of repairs. For example, if you have a vehicle that you are financing and your warranty is over, you are still responsible for the payments to the bank regardless of the fact that you may need a transmission. Even if you have a lemon law problem, this is totally separate from your obligation to the finance company. So you may be going back and forth with the dealer, but you still have the obligation to make the payment.

6. *Turn-ins.* Once you commit to a car note or lease and turn back the vehicle, you are then responsible for any deficiency. If you finance a 1998 vehicle, and it is sold for $10,000 at a forced sale, if $8,000 is still due on the loan, you owe the bank $8,000 and your credit is shot.

Finally

I am not saying that it is easy to pay cash for a vehicle, but if you make a mistake financing, there can be very negative implications, which put you in debt. Be careful before you tie yourself up with a commitment that you can't handle. If you "need" a car to show the world that you are a success then you may get sick inside trying to meet the payment obligations. Just as with a house, go over your budget for the last year — thoroughly. Also, to protect against illness or injury, inquire with your insurance agent about disability insurance to pay for the vehicle. Except in extreme cases, however, most people should have the ability to purchase a vehicle without financing.

Most people just don't understand the process of simplification. Between all the costs for additional auto insurance, substantial down payments, warranties and credit life insurance, you could have purchased a reliable vehicle that gets you from point A to point B. If you go through your budget and eliminate all unnecessary expenses, you will be able to accumulate enough cash to save and purchase your own vehicle and avoid the debt trap of financing. Remember the following points when considering financing a car:

- There is no tax benefit for financing.
- You will need increased auto insurance coverage, since you need complete coverage (and you must list the bank as a loss payee).
- Be sure you know the interest rate before financing.
- Financing destroys credit if there is a repossession or voluntary surrender.
- You are responsible for any money owed the bank if the vehicle is totaled or stolen, unless you have gap insurance.
- Dealers throw in a lot of unnecessary costs, such as credit life insurance and extended warranties, to boost the cost of the vehicle.
- Vehicles depreciate immediately. If you finance a vehicle for 60 months, you have the same payment when the vehicle has substantially decreased in value.

Chapter 4

Individual Rights and the Decline of Sacrifice

Our generation has lived in the greatest period of peacetime since the Second World War. With the advent of the counter culture of the sixties and seventies, the notion of loyalty to family, religion, country and other individuals has waned. After the Second World War, there was an incredible economic boom since there was an incredible demand for consumer goods after years of sacrifice. However, in conjunction with this economic boom came the expansion of individual rights which helped attack traditional values which held our country together.

How the Movement for Individual rights Hurt America

First, *Griswald v Connecticut*[1] denied the state from intruding on an individual's right to privacy. The right to privacy established in *Griswald v Connecticut* culminated in *Roe v Wade,*[2] which gave women the absolute right to terminate a pregnancy if it was done in the first trimester. There was also an expansion of individual rights in the criminal law arena, which emphasized the individuals right over society's right. As individual rights become more pronounced in matters of criminal law, sexual freedom and other first amendment rights, traditional values of loyalty, personal responsibility and sacrifice diminished. At the same time these social currents were occurring, the credit card emerged as the new status symbol, while the notion of saving — which used to be revered — has slipped away with other traditional value of loyalty, sacrifice and country.

The Vietnam War represented the first time there was a massive antiwar movement. Simultaneously, there was the advent of free love, civil rights and feminism. People began to lose the notion of duty, tradition, and loyalty and began to concentrate on individual rights and hedonism. As a result of this movement, people became more concerned with individual rights rather than a sense of honor, duty and service.

With the advent of individual rights, entitlements and the loss of sacrifice, duty and loyalty came the expansion of intermarriage. If one looks at the development of intermarriage in the United States, the figures are alarming. Fifty percent of all Japanese Americans and 52 percent of Jewish Americans intermarry. Also, intermarriage among Chinese Americans is on the rise. Similarly, among Italian Americans in the early 1960s, 59 percent of Italian Americans chose Americans of similar backgrounds; however, by 1979, the majority of Italian Americans were marrying people from outside their community. Also, more and more Italian Americans married out of their religious faith. Only 73 percent of the first generations married Catholics while 45 percent of the third generation did. In addition, the intermarriage rate is high for Irish and Polish Americans. Irish Americans intermarriage rate was 65 percent while the Polish American rate was 84 percent.[3]

In 1950, 57 percent of Christians disapproved of intermarriage with Jews while by 1983 only 12 percent of Protestants and 6 percent of Catholics were still against it.[4] It is true that this shows a tolerance; however, the flip side is that intermarriage shatters traditional values of group loyalty.

Elliot Abrams sums up the change in society and emphasis on individual autonomy as follows:

> The decision to put certain marriage partners off limits requires subordinating personal attraction and autonomy to other loyalties, usually to a racial or religious group and to a family's preferences. This is not the spirit of the age. The idea that one should sacrifice one's personal happiness to such old-fashioned considerations is a hard sell in America today. [5]

You may allege that the expansion of individual rights has absolutely no nexus to debt. It is true that many can argue that I have presented no evidence that expanded rights to privacy, expanded rights for criminal defendants and increased intermarriage creates debt. However, this book is about life choices and how they affect your financial future.

When individuals have a sense of loyalty, duty and honor, they think about other things before their own individual happiness. Thus, if someone is so interested in their own conception of romance that they give up their group for individual happiness, there is a greater chance that their own wants and needs will override in other areas of their life. It follows that, once the individual needs take over traditional values, there will be a financial impact. It is only logical that if you *must have* certain things, then eventually these things, wants and desires may cause financial disarray, if the other factors in this book come into play.

In essence, traditional values have held our country together. Once the expansion of individual rights begins to erode those values, these choices, as they interact with all the circumstances of life, may result in a debt trap for those who have given into hedonism.

The Power of Sacrifice

Another problem confronting the post-World War II generations is that we have never understood true sacrifice. We have never had to ration food or other material goods. So many parents have gone to extremes to give their children everything without being able to afford it. However, the media, Madison Avenue and the credit card companies have helped perpetuate the idea that you can have it all without earning it. Americans are used to getting whatever they want, when they want it, whether they can afford it or not. If you can't afford it, just put it on a credit card and worry about paying for it later. Don't worry if you can't buy that new luxury vehicle. You can lease it at $500 per month with absolutely no money down. Your job is your credit.

Americans have lost the idea of working to save and earn material goods. The lure of individual happiness overwhelms the thrill of saving to earn something and know it is yours — not the bank's. This extends to marriage, sexuality and psychology. The emphasis is to do what makes you happy, regardless of the impact it has on others. If you want the thrill of sex without the responsibility that goes with it (marriage, responsibility, love and covenant with God), that is your individual right. If you get pregnant because you didn't have "safe" sex, you can always get an abortion since you don't want the burden of having the responsibility of a child, regardless of the life that is being terminated. The key is that there is no longer the concept of sacrifice requiring people to take personal responsibility for their actions. As a result of the expansion of individual rights, people no longer value the ideals that made America the greatest country in the world. Due to the erosion of loyalty, duty and sacrifice, people have taken hedonism to the extreme and used debt to supplement their wants and desires.

People have to learn that sacrifice is essential for personal responsibility and a sense of self-fulfillment. It is time for people to grow up and realize that "you can't always get what you want."

Only when Americans get back to basics and earn their property from the fruits of their labor will they bring back the time-honored traditions that have worked in the past. In addition, the expansion of individual rights and decline of sacrifice has been the push for the external trappings of success.

You Are Not Entitled

As the country moved into a peacetime economy, manufacturers had to develop a market to sell. Also, after the scarcity and rations of the Second World War, there was a tremendous need for certain durable goods. However, with the rise in prosperity, many children of the World War II generations became disgusted with the old notions of tradition, family and hard work. However, the idealism of the sixties soon waned and many of the radicals of the sixties and seventies became the leaders of the present generation. With all the protests and drugs from the psychedelic era, these former protesters wanted all the goods that were now in the offering from the magnificent development in technology. The only difference was that the current generations never learned the notion of sacrifice but soon felt *entitled* to have all the material possessions.

There has been a direct correlation between developing a market and the demand for all these consumers' goods. However, it has come to a point at which Americans now have expectations that they are entitled to new cars, fancy toys and electronic products. It doesn't matter if they can afford them now; people can defer the payment and take care of it later. After the Second World War, there was an idea that started with the GI Bill that everyone should have equal opportunity. It is fine to give everybody an opportunity to get an education; however, this created a dumbing-down effect that lead everyone to believe that everyone should be *equal* rather than have *equal opportunity*.

As a result of this fundamental shift to everybody being equal, everyone feels that they are entitled to everything and there should be no differentiation, no matter how much you earn. Every child is supposed to be equal, since it is unfair to have some children feel better than others even though they have excelled in certain areas at a quicker pace. This notion of equality extends to material goods. Everyone feels entitled to own a home, regardless of whether they can afford the mortgage. They feel entitled to cars, which they cannot afford. People feel that their children are entitled to new clothing, separate bedrooms, TVs and all those other external trappings. There is nothing wrong, from a financial perspective, if you purchase all the consumer goods for you and your family — if you can afford it. However, when you are over your head in debt, then consumer goods are controlling your life.

The rise of bankruptcies in the 90s shows that our generation does not attach the same stigma to debt that prior generations did. This death of shame began in the counterculture of the sixties. People no longer worried about violating social norms, including dress, sexual behavior, drugs and violation of social standards that had persisted for thousands of years. With the sixties started the beginning of the breakdown of the family that has led to so many devastating social effects. Simultaneously, there was a breakdown of financial responsibility in conjunction with the breakdown of the social fabric. Along with free sex, came failure to take responsibility and increased debt when these fragile relationships broke. There is a direct correlation between financial responsibility and debt when there is no social responsibility.

Finally

People have to learn that they have to sacrifice their wants and not run up debt in order to satisfy their desires. Only when Americans get back to basics and earn their property from the fruits of their labor and savings will they bring back the time-honored traditions that have worked in the past.

Americans must get over the notion of just getting what they want without saving for it. Otherwise, we will have a society where bankruptcy is the norm and debt is considered a necessity since Americans want instant gratification. People will finance dinners, vacations, gambling, rock concerts and any other type of social matter if they do not have the money. The only way we are going to get above this debt mentality is to get back to fundamental ideas of sacrifice, savings and self-reliance. Only when Americans understand the notion of long term planning, savings and sacrifice will this debt cycle end.

Keep in mind the following points:

- The expansion of individual rights eroded old notions of sacrifice, duty and loyalty to country or tribe.
- The increase of intermarriage emphasized individual needs over traditional values.
- When individual rights are all-encompassing, desire for material needs leads to debt to meet those needs.
- The expansion of individual rights leads to a breakdown of sacrifice, resulting in more material desires, which leads to debt.
- The expansion of demand for entitlements creates debt.

Chapter 5

You're Approved

With the advent of individual rights, over the last forty years, came a simultaneous expansion of credit. In February 1999, consumer credit, which does not include loans secured by real estate, increased by an annualized rate of 7.9 percent in February 1999 by $1.3 trillion, according to the Federal Reserve. Automobile loans went up an annualized rate of 13.7 percent to $459 billion. That marked the fourth consecutive month in which car loans experienced a double-digit growth rate. Credit card debt is the largest segment of outstanding consumer debt, with individuals owing $569 billion on revolving credit accounts.[1]

Credit cards have been around since the early part of the twentieth century.[2] However, it was not until the 1950s that credit cards really expanded.[3] Credit cards have become an integral part of our society and, unfortunately, many ill-informed parents emphasize the notion of establishing credit, which puts their children into debt. Over my seventeen years of practice, I have seen how debt problems run in families.

Soliciting Debt

Today credit card companies do everything to solicit millions of people by giving them pre-approved cards at low introductory rates. They don't check to see your income and have sent credit cards to minors and people in nursing homes. The most amazing statistic is that credit card companies are actively soliciting high school students. As of 1993, 32 percent of high school students had credit cards.[4] The credit card companies are allegedly teaching financial management when there is a direct conflict of interest.[5] The only way to use a credit card is to write a check the same day that you used a credit card to make sure the money is there. Keep all your checks in a separate envelope and mail them to the credit card company when your bill comes due.

What is even more shocking is that credit card companies have lured 82 percent of full time college students with credit cards.[6] It appears that today the new rite of passage is obtaining credit cards. According to the US Public Interest Research Group, students who got credit cards through on campus sign ups are more likely to carry unpaid balances than students who get cards elsewhere. According to student loan providers, Nellie Mae, the median credit card debt was $1,222 and 14 percent of college students carried credit card debt of 3,000 – 7,000 dollars.[7] Representatives from MasterCard responded that 59 percent of students pay their balances in full each month compared with 40 percent of the general population.[8] It is absolutely amazing that only 40 percent of the general population and 59 percent of students pay their monthly balances in full.

What I have seen is that people who make only partial payments end up paying substantial interest rates. Soon the interest is getting so high that they are not putting a dent in principal.

Thus, 60 percent of the population is already falling into the debt trap by purchasing what they can't afford, while young people, who haven't even entered the job market, are already starting their adult lives in the red. I must note that the credit card companies are at least advising students to make their minimum monthly payments when they receive their bill.[9] However, they fail to advise the students that, after a while, the minimum monthly payments don't put a dent in principal. Eventually, even after making the minimum monthly payments you will get a demand for payment in full and then a lawsuit will follow.

How It Started

The major reason for the expansion of credit cards in the decade following World War II was due to the boom of an affluent and mobile society and the expansion of malls, suburban housing, motels TVs, highway systems and service station chains.[10] Credit cards were an integral part in fueling this boom. However, the other side of the coin is that credit cards have created a host of social problems ranging from rampant consumerism, indebtedness, dehumanization, crime, fraud, plus homogenization of the world's culture.[11]

Why have credit cards become so pervasive in our society? One major reason is that credit cards fuel the economy. They allow the economy to function at a much higher level since people spend faster than if they relied on cash and cashed-based instruments. Credit cards also help consumers increase their spending power, smooth out consumption when somebody is laid off or has no funds, and they're convenient. Merchants also benefit since they wouldn't get business if it weren't for the plastic.[12]

Credit cards have boomed because of their advantage over cash and checks. Cash can be stolen, lost or destroyed, while checks can be lost, stolen or destroyed. Also, cash can be counterfeited.[13] With the boom of credit cards has come a shift of attitudes toward debt. Savings used to be revered, but today debt is the password. "The status symbol of an ever increasing bank balance has been replaced by efforts to impress our friends with the magnitude of your mortgage loans and home equity lines of credit as well as the number of credit cards we possess and their upper limit."[14]

No Incentives for Savings

Since the government had a federal debt of $5.4 trillion in 2001, this doesn't encourage individuals to save. Furthermore, as government continues to overtax people, there is no basis for saving. The reason most families need both spouses to work today is that one spouse's income is necessary to absorb the huge tax crunch. Although individuals must take responsibility for their failure to save and control their materialistic desires, banks haven't helped with interest rates being so low. Also, while the government taxes on interest income the incentive to save has decreased. However, you can't solely blame the banks and government since there are many investment companies who give a fairly high rate of return but can't "guarantee" results.

The Lures

Besides sending pre-approved cards, credit card companies have expanded their business by using specific enhancements:

1. No annual fee
2. Rebates
3. Product discounts
4. Free insurance
5. Extended warranties
6. Exclusive access to special events

7. Free worldwide hotlines
8. Price protection
9. Gasoline
10. Air miles[15]

Most of these enhancements are difficult to take advantage of or offer very little to the consumer. The idea behind these enhancements is to create marketing value — not real value. The enhancements attract consumers, but most consumers don't use them.[16] However, if consumers revolve their accounts, they will not benefit from these enhancements and are better looking for a card with the lowest annual fee and lowest interest rate.[17]

The Plastic Trap

Why do people fall in the debt trap with credit cards? Instead of using their own common sense and budgeting techniques, they rely on the criteria used by banks in establishing an individual's credit line. The banks rely on an authorization mechanism that the consumer has reached his limit.[18] If the banks are such "experts" in establishing an individual's credit line, then why do 60 percent of all cardholders fail to pay their monthly balance in full?

The other problem is the intense solicitation that credit card companies use in sending pre-approved cards and only requiring minimum payments for statements. Part of the vicious cycle is that, once you get a credit card, you keep on getting more and more cards. A friend of mine represented a college student who was unemployed but got one pre-approved card. Since he had one card he was able to get other cards. Soon he took cash advances and bought a house free and clear. Because he was unemployed he was not able to pay on the credit card debts. However, home ownership allowed him to get a mortgage to pay off all the credit card debt. Since he had a mortgage, he got more pre-approved cards and used the cards to pay on the mortgage. This shows how easy it is to acquire debt without even employment since 82 percent of all full-time college students have credit cards.

Many senior citizens and other working class people who are struggling basically use the credit cards to pay for shelter, medicine and food. Senior citizens on fixed incomes are then trapped in this cycle with no way out except personal bankruptcy, which will be drastically changed if and when the pending bankruptcy legislation in Congress becomes law.

How Plastic Works

The credit card companies don't like consumers who pay their statements in full each month. However, they still get a cut from the vendor that accepts the credit cards. The banks get a double bonus for those 60 percent who don't pay their balances in full each month. They lure you with low "introductory" rates and then you get hit with a huge interest rate. They never tell you that $20 per month doesn't put a dent in principal and that it comes to a point when you are only paying back interest. The credit card companies don't tell you that it could take 22 years to pay back the debt at minimum payment of $36 per month.[19] Also, with the change of the tax laws, which eliminated a tax deduction for credit card interest in 1991, consumers have turned to home equity lines of credit which may give them a tax deduction and lower interest rate. However, home equity loans are not the answer.

If you default on a credit card debt, besides incurring negative credit, the bank can sue you, get a judgment, seize your property, garnish your wages or even get a lien on your real estate, if you own any. In contrast, if you default on a line of credit or home equity loan, you risk foreclosure. Studies have shown and I have seen that when consumers purchase new homes they are deluged with credit cards. Many people use the money as a self-esteem booster and lose sight that they will have to pay the debt back one day. If you use a credit card, make sure you write out the amount on a check that day and hold the checks until you get your monthly statement. If you are broke and must use the card for an emergency, use the card with the lowest interest rate and attempt to pay it off as soon as possible, before interest escalates. However, this should only be for an emergency.

It is true that many individuals have addictions and use credit cards to make themselves feel better. However, the banks go out of their way to keep you in this pattern of debt since they make a large profit. In 1995 total credit card debt was 195.2 billion (up 30 billion form June 1994).[20] Creditors get paid only from the vendor until you go into debt. Therefore, allegations that they are educating consumers about money management are clearly erroneous. Pay the statements in full.

In 1945 installment consumer debt was 2.5 billion. In 1955 it climbed to 29 billion, by 1965 it was 66 billion and by 1970 it was 100 billion. This does not include mortgage debt and noninstallment debt, such as charge accounts and bills for professional services. In 2000, total consumer debt was $1,569,000,000,000.[21] As of 1998, 44.1 percent of all U.S. families had credit card balances.

As a result of the increased credit, the economy has expanded because more money is available.

Between 1948 and 1967, bankruptcies increased from 16,000 filings to 191,000 filings [21] and over 1 million filings in 1997.[23] Between July 1, 2001, and June 30, 2002, 1,505,306 bankruptcies were filed and 1,466,105 of the filings were consumer filings.[24]

The reason for dysfunction in consumer credit is two fold. Installment credit has led to fraudulent and deceptive marketing, which can't be done on a cash basis. The second reason is that regulation is the failure of the law to keep up with the changes. It was bad on commercial law, which regulated business. Once consumers sign a contract of adhesion, they are stuck.[25]

Reasons for Failure to Pay

One major reason for nonpayment of obligation is a change in the debtor's marital status.[26] Another reason for debt is misplaced trust in a friend or relative.[27] For example, if you co-signed for someone who defaulted, you are responsible. Also, debtors get into trouble if they trust the wrong person to make payments on their bills.

This study showed that the major reason of nonpayment is loss of income from negative change in employment status — such as loss of job, shorter work week or unemployment during a strike.[28] With the current climate of downsizing, most people have tied themselves to commitments that don't work. People fail to be a step ahead to anticipate possible loss of income.

You have free will and you have to deal with the temptation offered by the credit card companies. The credit card companies go out of their way to make you their customer since the credit card business is 3 or 4 times more profitable than banks.[29] Besides the incentives offered, credit cards are safer than cash, they give you stop payment rights, extended warranties, plus they delay payment until the bill becomes due.[30] Credit card companies earn 2-10 percent from the merchant (store)[31] plus a huge amount of interest from the 60 percent of Americans that don't pay their balances in full each month. The banks are making huge profits when they are paying 1 or 2 percent to savers and make 18-21 percent interest on credit card customers who don't pay their bills timely.[32] Also, merchants prefer credit cards since they believe they are getting bigger profits.[33]

Unfortunately, very few Americans really understand the purpose of a credit card (i.e. to avoid carrying large amounts of cash and giving you other safety protection plus possible enhancements). Most people live in this instant gratification mode without planning for the long term. Will I still have my same job and income level in 5 years? Will I have additional children? Will I have unforeseen medical expenses? The old adage of saving for a rainy day no longer exists because people want everything yesterday. People don't want to delay sexual gratification or material pleasures. We live in a hedonistic society where credit cards let you get whatever you want without having to save. There is no longer any satisfaction for working to save for an item.

People look at finances with tunnel vision and figure that since they are getting 20 hours overtime now; they will get it forever. Meanwhile, they tie themselves to long-term financial commitments without realizing that if the overtime dries up or the job is downsized, there is a debt to be paid. People want to have everything now and assume that they will always have the money to make payments to satisfy their hedonistic lifestyles.

It takes a great deal of self-control when you hear all the ads on radio and TV: NO MONEY DOWN, YOU'LL DRIVE HOME IN A NEW CAR; CREDIT PROBLEMS ARE NO PROBLEM; NO PAYMENTS FOR ONE YEAR; GIVE YOURSELF A RAISE BY REFINANCING; and all the other gimmicks. How do you resist the pre-approved cards with $10,000 limits and "checks" for $5,000, $10,000 and even more? You have free will, so consider all the implications before you incur the debt.

I have seen clients who, within six months after getting a bankruptcy discharge, fall behind on their mortgage and car payments plus incur additional credit card debt. One client incurred over $60,000 credit card debt within four years after a bankruptcy discharge. People must learn to revert to what most people learned growing up. Unless you have the cash, you don't have the money to purchase it. If you use credit cards, pay if off the same day by writing a check; or if an emergency strikes, pay if off in full after you receive the bill. You will be held responsible.

Beware of the plastic loan shark.[34] Once you get suckered in, you will only get deeper and deeper in debt. If you are a college student with debt, this may affect future job prospects or a mortgage in the future.

The other signs that you are in the debt trap are as follows:

1. *Making minimum payments.* This doesn't put a dent in principal and may not even cover interest. This will enlarge your debt;
2. *Getting cash advances to satisfy other debts.* This shows there is a problem since you can't meet your existing obligations;
3. *Purchasing groceries on credit.* This is clear evidence that you can't afford your lifestyle, unless you do this to get enhancements;
4. *Having no money left at the end of the month.* This shows you are living beyond your means;
5. *Seeking a debt consolidation loan.* This is not the answer since after getting a consolidation loan, you end up incurring more debt;
6. *If credit cards are "maxed out" you draw on home equity lines of credit.* This is extremely dangerous since you put your home at risk;
7. *Not opening letters from credit card companies.* This is a sure sign of denial.[35]

If you can resist the initial temptation then you will avoid the debt trap. Once you get into this trap, it will be a lot harder to get out.

Chapter 6

The Three Rs and Budgeting

Since we were little kids our schools taught us reading, writing and arithmetic. The problem is that no grade schools, middle school, high school, college or graduate school actually prepares people for budgeting their expenses in the real world.

When you were a kid, your parents may have given you a weekly allowance. If you were given $5.00 per week, you knew that you couldn't buy a gift for $20.00 until you saved four weeks of allowance. The problem is that most Americans know how much they earn but have no conception what they spend in a month.

Lying to Yourself About Costs

To stay debt free you must have the commitment to save, be willing to sacrifice and practice defensive spending. It will not be productive unless you know not only what your expenses are, but what monthly expenses are necessities for your survival. I have met thousands of clients who don't have any idea of how much they spend. Several people even asked me how much their mortgage payment was.

Families with four children will tell me they spend $300.00 per month on groceries and $50.00 per month on clothing. People frequently claim never to have any medical expenses or repairs for their cars or home. Clients will rarely admit that they spend a great deal of their take home income for recreation (i.e. eating out, alcohol, tobacco, gambling, and vacations).

If a person grosses $10.00 per hour and makes $400.00 per week, he will only take home around $312.00 per week after subtracting federal tax, Social Security, and state tax and disability tax. Many people have additional deductions for health insurance, 401K, pension, pension loans and other deductions that substantially reduce their net pay.

It is essential that you take the time to write down all of your regular monthly expenses. If they are too high, based on your net income, you have to either cut out the nonnecessities or generate additional income.

Reality-based Expenses

Let's carefully examine a family's expenses. The standard costs that should never fluctuate are costs for shelter (i.e. rent or mortgage), utilities, electric and gas, oil, water, sewer, trash and cable TV. These expenses may fluctuate depending on how the family chooses to use these resources.

People rarely ever anticipate major home expenses. For families who have no savings and live from pay check to pay check, one major home repair, or similarly a major car repair, will create a shortfall that will result in them getting behind in other bills, which can have a devastating chain-reaction effect.

Food

Everybody has to purchase groceries to survive. Many clients I come into contact with either substantially underestimate their food budget (as with the family who claimed to spend only $300.00 per month for a family of five) or overestimate it (as with families who claim to spend $800.00 per month for a family of four) These families are, most likely, living way above their means. People all need healthy food for sustenance, plus paper products and other sundries. People have to decide what is necessary and within their limits in allocating how much they spend on groceries. In determining the grocery budget, also determine what you spend for all the snacks, junk food and eating out to view the total picture

Clothing

It is necessary for everyone to have basic clothing. Families must decide what is reasonable. Many are able to purchase good, quality clothing at a reasonable price while others need designer clothing to satisfy their egos. This is one expenditure over which the individual has a great deal of control.

Laundry and Dry cleaning

Laundry costs are usually included in expenses for groceries (detergent and fabric softener) and electricity (to power the washer and dryer). Professional people may need to dry clean their clothing for their employment, and they must remember to include such costs in their expenses.

Medical

This is one budgeting item that is outside of your control. It is fundamental that you have health insurance to protect yourself from medical catastrophes. People can't always plan medical expenses, dental expenses and other unanticipated costs, which are necessities. As with other planning techniques, it is necessary to try to anticipate co-payments for normal medications, doctor visits and anticipated medical services.

Transportation

The costs of transportation will vary substantially depending on the type of car, commute and car payments, if any. Some people are naturally going to have to spend a much larger amount on transportation expenses due to the distance they commute for their job. Further, fuel economy should be an important consideration in expenses. Safety is a natural concern, but you have to look at all of the risks versus all of the benefits in budgeting for transportation expenses.

If you wish to drive a large, luxury vehicle, the cost for gasoline, parts and labor are going to be substantially more than upkeep for an economy car. However, this is a choice each individual must determine in examining a budget.

Recreation

Money spent on recreational costs can make a major difference in an individual's net worth. In *Anthony Robbins Personal Power*, Mr. Robbins explains that if you save $3.25 per day — perhaps the amount you spend on cigarettes, for example — the money could be worth $75,000 after 25 years with a 16 percent rate of return.[1]

Americans never seem to consider the money that they spend on cigarettes, snacks, eating out and vacations, which gives them no taxable benefit. Also, since we pay over one-third of our income for taxes, a large portion of the take home income that we generate is depleted. Each week, 7.65 percent is taken out of your paycheck for Social Security, and federal taxes eat up a large percentage of your income regardless of your tax bracket. Also, the state government takes out taxes plus SDI and Medicare. Other people may have health insurance, pension, loans, 401K, profit sharing and a host of other deductions from their take-home pay. Therefore, you should be very careful about how much you spend on recreation, entertainment and newspapers. If you actually add this to the necessary expenses, then it becomes obvious how you could very easily fall into debt.

Even if you have a substantial surplus in your budget, you should never sit on your laurels. For every dollar you save on recreation, work out a plan and get good investment brokers, and your money will accumulate substantially over a period of time. Anthony Robbins goes further in his analysis and states that if you save $200 per month at the same rate of return, the money could be worth almost $1 million in 25 years.[2]

Charity

It is essential that people give back to the community in the form of charitable contributions. Without charity many worthwhile organizations that fight illness or help people in need would not survive. You should emphasize helping only one charity that is near and dear to your heart. If your budget is tight and you cannot afford financial contributions, you should give of your time.

Not all charities are the same; be careful that the charity uses most of its money toward the cause. Unfortunately, unbeknownst to many, certain charities pay large administrative expenses to salaried employees, and your contribution may be helping John Smith earn a $80,000 salary as chief fund raiser for said charity.

Insurance

Insurance is one of the most important expenses you have. If you don't have insurance it can severely compromise your financial integrity. I have seen many people whose lives have been destroyed financially because of having no insurance. Regardless of the fact if you own or rent a home, insurance is essential. If there ever is a fire, burglary or act of God, you can be devastated financially without insurance. Most mortgage companies pay homeowners insurance to protect their interest in the property. However, if you have any expensive property, you should get a rider on your policy to protect jewelry and/or other assets.

Most renters don't understand how important it is to protect property in a rental dwelling. The cost is much lower than homeowners insurance, but it is still necessary to protect yourself against burglaries or acts of God.

Life insurance is also imperative. If you don't have a lot of cash presently and are in good health, you can purchase term life insurance to protect your family at a minimal cost. On the other hand, if you are planning for the long term and wish to build a cash surrender, then you can purchase whole life insurance.

Auto insurance is imperative for persons who drive since a car accident can lead to devastating financial consequences. If you don't have proper coverage, a judgment can be entered against you and you may not only lose your driver's license but you can lose your home and any other assets you might own. Most states require auto insurance as mandatory under their motor vehicle statues; however, you must make sure you are adequately insured so a large judgment won't ruin you. The increased cost of insurance is minimal compared to the risk of not having proper insurance in the case of an accident.

It is advisable not to skimp on minimum insurance since you can lose your property if you have only minimum coverage. Also, I would strongly advise uninsured and underinsured insurance to cover you if you are seriously injured by a party who has no insurance or who has minimum insurance and is judgment proof.

Finally, you must determine any other additional monthly expenses involving your children, such as daycare, baby-sitting, school expenses, gifts, birthday parties and any other potential expenses.

One of the worst mistakes homeowners make is their failure to anticipate home repairs and/or car repairs. Unfortunately, there is no fixed amount of money for these expenses. However, if you are living above your means and there is a major unanticipated repair bill, it can have a domino effect and set you behind on all other expenses. The best way to prepare for unforeseen circumstances when you buy a home is not to use every penny for your down payment and have some savings available for unexpected repairs. If you are purchasing a home, please take precautions to anticipate these types of challenges.

I recommend that you go over your budget thoroughly before you decide where you want to live, if you wish to finance a vehicle or any other item. The key is to plan in advance and live within your means. If you anticipate additional income or intangibles it will help prevent additional debt. Remember that without an initial understanding of how much you spend and how much you bring in, you are doomed to a life of debt.

Review your budget thoroughly for the last year. Analyze your yearly expenditures for fixed expenses and expenses that vary, such as repairs, maintenance, medical, recreation, gifts and any other potential expenses.

If you don't know exactly what your take-home pay and average monthly expenses are, you will become a victim of the debt trap.

Chapter 7

You Owe It To Me

The *Great Society* under President Johnson was intended to bring a lot of good social programs and wage a War on Poverty. Unfortunately, as the government kept on pouring more money into social welfare programs, sexual education programs and job training, crime rates increased, teenage pregnancies rose and an entire generation of welfare recipients became entrenched in a new class in society. As more people became dependent on government, fewer and fewer people began taking responsibility for their lives.

America has now become a nation of victims. People feel they are entitled to social security, unemployment insurance, medical coverage, food stamps and several other entitlements. The notion of personal responsibility has disappeared. I think it is time that people follow songwriter Don Henley's advice and "Get Over It."

It's Not My Fault, I'm a Victim

Unemployment insurance was not supposed to be a six-month vacation for people. It was a stopgap provision to assist people while they lost their job. There is something wrong when teenagers who live at home get unemployment. The notion of entitlement goes way beyond government social welfare programs. Nobody wants to take responsibility for their actions and always want to find somebody to blame. People don't seem to realize that we all have free will and that the circumstances of our lives result from the choices that we have voluntarily made.

If somebody is injured, there is always somebody else to blame and sue. If you get drunk and injure yourself, it is the bar's responsibility since they kept on serving you even though you knew you couldn't see straight. If a man loses his job, it must be because of discrimination; merit is never considered. If you don't get into a certain school it must be because the admission tests are biased. If you fail to make your mortgage payments, it is the government's responsibility to pay for your shelter. If you total you car, it is the manufacturer's fault that the car wasn't crashworthy. If you purchase hot coffee and drive your car, it is the restaurant's responsibility if you burn yourself. Finally, even if someone commits crimes of murder, rape, aggravated assault and any other conceivable crime, it is a mitigating factor that you were abused as a child.

Another example was the Rodney King debacle. Looting and destruction was allowed because the fabric of our society created these conditions. Unfortunately, we live in an age where we have created a society of victims. The emergence of this entitlement mentality permeates society in all aspects. This entitlement mentality has expanded to the notion of "I am entitled to anything I want even if I cannot afford it." This notion of individual rights without regard for personal responsibility can be seen in all areas of the economy. Even though you can't afford to buy the brand new Mercedes Benz, you can afford to lease it since you have credit and a good paying job. The media has created this notion that we have a right to anything we want. Since the banks, through their experts, know exactly how much we can afford, then almost anything is within reach.

The media expands this victim mentality by making it our God given right to use the equity in our home for a vacation, remodeling or anything our little heart desires. We are entitled to everything. If our doctors don't solve all our problems, they committed malpractice even though they explained the risks. If our lawyer didn't put every single point in writing, he is responsible for all of our misfortunes.

- "We didn't know we had to resume our mortgage payment, car payment or any other payment."

- "I am current on my mortgage payment on March 29, 2001, since I have paid through February."

- "I never got your letters."

- "You never returned my call."

These are all examples of the victim mentality and blame game that permeates our litigation-oriented society.

The key is personal responsibility in all areas of your life. If you miss work, you are not entitled to free time. If you make a mistake, correct it for the consumer at no charge. Have pride in what you do. Responsibility is the backbone of a strong financial condition. If you have an entitlement mentality without truly examining the numbers, you are not taking personal responsibility. If you fail to plan, then you have definitely planned to fail.

Most people never plan for emergencies, business set backs, slow periods or other circumstances that reduce their income. I have seen people who had six-figure incomes who are overwhelmed by debt because they never planned for emergencies.

Life is made up of joy and woe, good and bad, and too many people fail to save for the rainy days.

So many people want to find someone else to blame. Remember that life is made up of all our choices, for which we are totally responsible. We are not only destroying ourselves but we are destroying society with that "you owe it to me" mentality. Unfortunately, the media feeds on the victim mentality. There are constant barrages of ads encouraging people to sue doctors whenever something goes wrong. I am not saying that professionals never err; however, a society cannot operate in an environment in which people refuse to take responsibility for their choices.

As long as we feel that we are entitled to everything, the traditional mentality of the Protestant work ethic is destroyed. Besides the anger and the hatred and rage, which has become commonplace, it destroys personal responsibility. Once personal responsibility falls, debt emerges and "It's not my fault." The victimization of American Society destroys the robustness of our economy and destroys incentive and risk because nobody wants to take responsibility. Minimize your damages and move on with your life.

Keep in mind these points:

- Since the *Great Society*, America has become a nation of victims.
- People feel entitled to a host of social welfare programs.
- People don't take responsibility for their choices and always try to blame somebody through a lawsuit.
- There is the notion that we have the right to anything we want, regardless of whether we can afford it.
- Take responsibility for your choices.

Chapter 8

If It Makes You Feel Good

Madison Avenue spends enormous sums of money annually selling you every conceivable service or material good under the sun. When you see an advertisement for a cigarette, you are usually being sold attractive men or women, beautiful landscapes, or freedom-inducing images that have nothing to do with cigarettes. The cigarette itself usually has a bitter taste and doesn't come with beautiful girls or gorgeous islands. However, the advertising gurus are selling sex, pleasure and freedom rather than cigarettes.

Making You Want It

The larger problem is the push for financing that is so prevalent in advertising today. Consumers are trapped into promises of instant gratification.

NO MONEY DOWN

NO PAYMENTS FOR 1 YEAR

NO CREDIT–NO PROBLEM

Next they work on your aesthetic sense by showing a sexy female driving a flashy looking vehicle. Advertisers will rarely advertise price because most consumers cannot come up with $20,000 to purchase a new vehicle. Most advertisers, after selling the vehicles, jewelry, or other items through aesthetics, will then emphasize *payments* that focus on the short term rather than the actual cost that focuses on long-term planning. For example, you can lease a $40,000 vehicle for *only* $499 a month and have all the luxury and comforts immediately without having to save for the vehicle. Madison Avenue doesn't care whether you can afford the vehicle as long as you buy or lease the vehicle.

Most consumers I've dealt with do not read and have no conception of the interest rate or equity in the vehicle. The bottom line is the $250 or $499 per month, which is what they feel is affordable to them. There is no consideration of the interest rate. All that matters is that you have a "reliable" means of transportation. People don't consider the additional costs of financing as long as they feel "the payment" fits within their budget.

Are You a Sucker?

Madison Avenue has played on the instant gratification theme by pushing for uses of credit cards, since they allegedly make you more mature, successful and worldly. Also, they give you unlimited opportunity to go anywhere or do anything. There is no longer any emphasis on payments, interest rate and length of time paying back a credit card. Consumers don't understand that $50 per month can take years to pay back because the minimal monthly payments will not put a dent in the principal amount.

Everybody has some hidden yearning that they were deprived of growing up. Madison Avenue has an answer for everyone. If you have issues with self-esteem, an exciting vehicle will make you more "macho." You are not being sold the vehicle; you are being sold images, success, sexual prowess and other mind games that have nothing to do with the vehicle.

The problem then moves to the second tier. Madison Avenue has got your interest and now you go to the dealer or retail outlet. People are never truly told how much they are paying for an item because everything is reduced to a monthly payment. Very few consumers realize that most items, when they leave the store, start depreciating immediately. However, so many people are caught up with the mentality of wearing the right clothes and driving the right car that they don't look at the implications.

In and of itself, Madison Avenue is just doing a job of selling items or services. The problem occurs when people get so caught up with their life styles that it drives them into staggering debt. Once the debt trap hooks you, you are caught. In a society where three out of every five Americans can't pay their credit card bills each month, this is an extremely dangerous phenomena.

The unfortunate part is that Madison Avenue doesn't just sucker the kids who are naïve and don't know better; older people still get caught up on this ride and find themselves in substantial debt since they couldn't control themselves. Remember, if something sounds too good to be true, it probably is. What business in their right mind would give you a new television or stereo system at no payments and no interest for a year without protecting themselves with a security agreement in the collateral plus a huge interest rate after the free period elapses?

Nothing Is Free

It amazes me how much people are suckered with the word FREE. Any business that does things for free is doomed to failure since in a capitalistic economy profit is the motive. This doesn't mean that service and quality don't exist, it means that nothing is FREE. Most people refuse to read and look at the short-term fix rather than the long-term solution.

It truly amazes me how we are all flooded with pre-approved credit cards with low introductory rates. These are not gifts that we can defer forever. After the bank gets you hooked, then the interest rate goes up to over 20 percent. However, most people don't worry since they claim they are "current" with all their payments. I still cringe when people come into my office with over $100,000 in credit card debt on their shoulder and tell me they are current. If they are making minimal payments, it could take them years to pay back the debt. However, the problem is not with the massive debt the people procure, but with why they are seduced into obtaining all this credit. People have to learn that instant gratification is not the answer.

Be Realistic

Many Americans don't seem to understand cause and effect. Every choice you make is a cause and if you let your mind play games with you, you will lose control and let the negative effect of debt destroy you. It is certainly tempting when you have had a slow down or layoff to cash a $10,000 "check" from a credit card company. What is the "cash" you received? It has now attached as a mortgage onto your property. What about the stereo equipment, TVs and computers you purchase from the appliance store? Consumers don't realize that many stores are now taking security interests in the collateral. This means that if you don't pay they can repossess it.

The problem is that when you combine the mentality of "you can have everything" with sophisticated businesses, most consumers get caught in poor deals when they think they are getting something for FREE. Why are people paying the equivalent of a few thousand dollars for a big-screen TV when they can purchase it in cash for a much lesser price? Americans have to stop looking at the short term payments and look at the total cost.

I am not saying that it is easy with all the peer pressure and societal norms to look good, feel good and keep up with the Jones'. You have to be stronger and know what you can afford; otherwise you will hit the slippery slope and free fall into a life of debt, stress and abdication of personal responsibility. If people begin to value themselves rather than their job, car, clothing, home or other material possessions, they will avoid the trap of debt, which is fed by Madison Avenue.

Refinancing Isn't the Answer

The other dangerous trend is refinancing. If you turn on the television, you will see numerous commercials about no mortgage payments for three months, give yourself a raise, save hundreds of dollars a month. Most people think that this simple procedure will resolve all issues. The problem is that first refinancing isn't free: there are a lot of additional costs and expenses for refinancing — with no guarantee.

First, there is usually a nonrefundable application fee; second, there may be several judicial liens on the property that have to be satisfied; finally, many people will refinance without satisfying a great deal of debt. Thus, after refinancing, people may find themselves still in debt.

However, the major problem is not the refinancing, it goes back to poor budgeting. Even if somebody can reduce their mortgage payment by $500 per month, there will still be issues of inability to budget. If you think that the simple answer is refinancing a mortgage that you have $10,000 arrears, you are totally missing the point. Just because you suddenly have a new mortgage payment doesn't resolve the cause of the problem; poor budgeting or living above your means. If you refinance and truly work out a payment within your means whereby you are not living paycheck by paycheck then refinancing is an option.

The other problem with Madison Avenue is that people think they have a right to have anything they want regardless of their true need or ability to pay. If you can't afford the item, then you can always finance it by a credit card, or with many items you won't have to make payments for six months or one year. There will be no interest or payments until that payment period begins. However, you are never told that, once the payments kick in, the interest rates can be substantial.

Also, with these deals, the ordinary consumer doesn't realize that the store has a lien on these items under the Uniform Commercial Code. For example, Sears takes a purchase money security interest on many items to protect its interest in case of a bankruptcy filing; this elevates Sears to the status of a secured creditor rather than a general unsecured creditor. What this means is that if you fail to make payments on a secured debt, the creditor can repossess your collateral.

The other issue is that you can charge as many items as you want and just make minimal payments for years. This will soon lead to financial disaster since you will be paying interest for years without satisfying the principal. The other alternative is that even if Madison Avenue does not eat up your credit cards; it will take money away from savings and investment, which will hurt you in the long run.

Finally

In essence, it is necessary that all of us have items for our necessity. The fear is that if you let Madison Avenue control all your spending then you will have a major financial dilemma. Keep in mind these points when considering the purchase of feel-good items:

- Madison Avenue sells youth, beauty, sex and freedom.
- There is emphasis on payment rather than the true cost of the product.
- Watch out for "FREE." Nothing is free in a capitalistic society where profit is the motive.
- Many stores, such as Sears, take security interests in appliances and other consumer goods. This means that if you don't make payments, the collateral can be repossessed.
- Refinancing isn't the answer if you don't budget right or if you live above your means.

Chapter 9

Take Responsibility for Your Choices and Bills

I can tell you hundreds of stories of clients who didn't pay their bills because a friend, spouse, brother, nephew, you name it, was supposed to pay the bill. When you sign any type of contract such as a mortgage, car note or credit card, *you* are responsible for the bill. You should not take on responsibility if you cannot afford the payment and have to rely on a third person to assist you. If you go out of town and give your brother the mortgage payments and he spends it on his own recreational activities, don't be surprised if you get a foreclosure notice.

One Should Do It

The unfortunate situation is when a spouse or partner runs up credit and fails to make payments. However, we have to learn from our mistakes. We must try to view life as a chess game whereby we have to think a few moves in advance for those emergencies we all bump into. However, if you live with somebody who has a gambling, drinking or other problem, take charge of the books. One person in the family should take personal responsibility for paying the joint bills. Otherwise, there will be financial chaos since you won't know how much is in the other party's checkbook or what outstanding checks exist.

Agree to Be Responsible

It is my position that when two people are connected either by the bonds of matrimony or any other type of relationship they must also be financial partners. There must be an agreed upon groundwork before you start incurring joint obligations. I have seen too many people who were left holding the bag when the girlfriend or boyfriend, who were supposed to contribute to the mortgage, left. This is why it is so important that people weigh all their financial choices before they commit to signing the dotted line. Remember, once you are a co-signer, you may be 100 percent responsible for the bill if the other party defaults.

It is my opinion that you should never rely on another person's income since you are creating too many variables. However, couples who budget well and are most successful financially work well as a team.[1] If you rely on your own income to cover a mortgage payment, or any other expense, then you put yourself in more control over the debt trap. If an unfortunate circumstance occurs outside of your control, then the spouses or significant other's income can help out. But it is advisable not to liquidate all of your assets — have some savings to protect yourself.

Life's uncertainties cause so many first-time homebuyers to fall into trouble. If you work as a team, you can scrutinize your income and expenses to get a true grasp of what's coming in and going out. Unfortunately, sometimes you misanticipated and created a situation where you are barely making it on income. But if you work together, you can make some modifications on expenses since a lot of expenses are well within your control. Each month you have certain fixed expenses that you can't control. However, utilities, food, clothing and entertainment can certainly be modified to accommodate the changed financial situation.

Don't Have Fun at the Expense of Your Financial Future

There is certainly nothing wrong with using a certain amount of money for fun: sporting events, vacations, entertainment, shows, etc. However, if you are in debt, you are creating a major mistake in spending your money on entertainment, when you are behind on other bills. I believe in freedom, and even though I think cigarettes don't promote health, it is your freedom as an American to smoke cigarettes. I just don't understand how people can spend $200 per month on cigarettes and another $100 on "clubs" per month when they are behind on their mortgage, credit cards or other financial obligations.

> *You must reexamine your budget before spending money on "fun" items.*

But you think it is unfair that your kids can't go to this game and/or event or that you deserve a couple of beers with the boys. The best line I heard was, "I had to give my kids a Christmas." Let me ask you, is it better to give your kids a secure home in a decent neighborhood with minimal gifts for Christmas, or is it better to give them a lot of gifts that will probably bore them after a while, while the bank is ready to foreclose on their home? Many people in this country just miss the true meaning of religious celebrations. Isn't the true meaning of Christmas the religious significance of Jesus Christ's birth rather than materialism? Isn't the religious significance of a bar mitzvah or bat mitzvah the idea of the young man or woman taking on responsibility in the Jewish religion, rather than gifts or parties?

Why would people take out a loan to pay for a wedding, Bar Mitzvah or other religious celebration? A wedding (hopefully) is only one day, just as a Bar Mitzvah. Is it fair for people to put themselves into debt for these occasions or for Christmas? Isn't the true spirit of the religious event the love, faith, and *responsibility* that comes with your religion? What would Jesus say if he saw you bankrupting your home in order to buy the fanciest gifts for your children at Christmas? What would your great-grandfather, who left Eastern Europe to find religious freedom, say if he knew you took a home equity loan to finance a Bar Mitzvah? People just refuse to take responsibility for these decisions and continuously want to keep up with the "Jones'" or have instant gratification.

Sometimes, Things Just Happen

This book is not a guarantee. No matter how hard you try you may hit bumps such as loss of job, illness or serious accidents. But you have to try to save for a rainy day and anticipate. It is not the government's responsibility when you lose your job, or depended on overtime to pay for your mortgage, car payment or credit cards. The extra money you were earning should have been used for paying down debt. However, too many people *depend* on overtime or *assume* that things will always stay the same.

Most people I have dealt with refuse to save for the rainy day. They assume that things will always be constant or, once they have hit hard times, that things will always be bad. Life is made of ups and downs. However, if things were never bad, people could never appreciate the good. You must learn to deal with financial difficulties to bless the good times; but if you always expect things to be easy financially, without ever having suffered hard times, you will never have built character.

If You Fail to Plan, You Plan to Fail

Whether you are self-employed or get a paycheck, you must have a strategy. Those who fail to have a budget fail to stay out of debt. Again, over and over people in debt think that getting another "loan" will get them out of debt. You would be amazed at the number of persons who seek to finance a vehicle at unbelievable interest rates after they have been discharged from bankruptcy or are currently in a plan of reorganization. Again, they fail to consider the quality, safety and only look at the initial payment not realizing that they may be paying for a vehicle twice as much as its worth instead of saving for a pre-owned vehicle.

People also try to get out of debt by taking loans at 30 percent interest rates to consolidate debts and give all their personal property as collateral. This means that the finance company has a lien on the property if you don't pay the loan. In our instant-gratification society people feel they are "entitled" to own a home, regardless of the mortgage, entitled to a new car and entitled to all the "good" things in life whether they can afford it. The whole concept of paying your dues no longer seems to apply. If people have too many children, the government provides Medicaid, food stamps and free lunches. People must take responsibility for their choices.

Years ago, many people had larger families and were poor, but families pooled their resources and still had values without unrealistic expectations. People no longer have to worry about choices that they make especially concerning financial matters since bankruptcy is always an option to clean the slate. However, with the pending bankruptcy reform legislation, this may no longer be the case.

People no longer seem to associate stigmas with certain behaviors. When I was growing up, if a person had a child out of wedlock it was kept hush-hush and the family took care of the child. Now, so many people "have" families without the benefit of marriage, and there appears to be the same pattern of failure to plan socially as there is financially. Life is hard enough when you work to raise a family and attempt to pay the bills. However, if you fail to plan regarding family, then you will find yourself out of control since your budget will be out of whack, and you will not be able to keep up with the necessities, let alone the additional unexpected bills. If you don't take personal responsibility for your actions, unbelievable problems will develop.

A Loan Is No Cure

I met an extremely successful musician who was in the millionaires' club in the 1980s. Unfortunately, he never prepared for the ups and downs of life and soon found he was in financial disarray, and his home was in foreclosure. Mr. Musician was attempting to rebound from the days of glory and needed a loan to help him with expenses on his current compact disc release. He relied on unscrupulous people who told him that "they would take care of him." What was supposedly a $47,000 loan became a $63,000 lease of all his equipment and a second mortgage on his property — payable in five years with 18 percent interest.

I have seen others who feel that loans are the answer for everything. The problem is a lot of the loan officers never really consider whether the applicant has the ability to pay. People who are disabled, unemployed and have no ability are given loans because of equity in their home, when they have absolutely no ability to pay. The other option is people take loans while giving all their personal property as collateral. If they don't pay the loan, all their personal property can then be seized.

If people just accept to live within their means and take responsibility for their actions, they will not get themselves in this dilemma.

Finally

When considering your financial responsibilities, consider the following points:

- You are solely responsible for any debt. Don't rely on anyone else to pay it except for your financial partner.

- If you work well with your financial partner, you will be more successful financially.

- Don't get into debt for Christmas or other special occasions, such as Bar Mitzvahs, communions or weddings.

- You must save for the rainy day because there are bumps in life's road.

- If you don't budget, you plan to fail.

- Loans are not a solution to debt without understanding the reason you got into debt. You have to deal with the root of the problem rather than relying on a loan as a quick-fix solution.

Chapter 10

Don't Gamble On It

No matter how defensive a spender you are and how frugal you are with saving, if you have a gambling problem you will never live a life without debt. I have seen so many people fall substantially behind on their mortgage payments and/or run up substantial credit card debt for cash advances because they had a serious gambling problem. (This would also apply to people who have alcohol or drug addictions.) If you want to go to the casinos and gamble, allocate the amount of money that you can afford to lose and use that for a night of entertainment.

If It Sounds Too Good to Be True...

People are so obsessed with making quick money that, instead of taking $100 per month toward investing, they will use that money on lottery tickets, the horses, or football pools.

Football Pools

Unfortunately, more people are concerned with the point spread rather than the actual sporting event. Millions of dollars are risked on football pools each year. Again, the money spent on pools every weekend costs an individual money that he would have had to pay his bills.

It is okay to gamble if you have control over your funds. However, you can save a lot more money by investing the money you would have used for gambling, rather than using it for gambling.

It is the rare occurrence that gambling hits a jackpot that will clear you from debt.

The Lottery

People spend substantial sums searching for the big jackpot. Lately there has been Powerball where $100 million jackpots have been advertised. People are so allured by money that they use up a lot of money that they could have used for investments toward an extremely slim opportunity to hit a large jackpot. If you save that money and invest $100 per month, you can save *thousands* of dollars over the years.

Even investing too heavily in the lottery can damage people. Sure, you hear of the news of people winning the lottery; however, such a small percentage of people win that your chances are extremely slim. If you are betting on the lottery to lift you out of debt, you had better take another course of action.

Finally

If you are living in a dream world in which you are going to make a big hit from gambling and get caught up with all your debts, please know that it will rarely happen. If people can win gambling, then why do casinos nationally make such huge profits and employ so many people? For the average working man, gambling can be a serious problem that can lead to financial devastation. I have seen too many people lose all material possessions because of a gambling problem.

The racetrack is similar to casinos, football pools or the lottery. Your chance of hitting it big from the racetrack is rare. Unfortunately, many people get addicted and lose their life savings or get in substantial debt by running up the credit card.

There is absolutely nothing wrong with playing the lottery, horses, football pool or the casino if you have control and have set limits. The problem is when the gambling becomes an addiction and you don't know when to stop. When you are using your mortgage payment to pay for your gambling addiction or keep on running up the cash advances on the credit card, you must get some type of counseling. Gambling is an illness, like alcoholism, that must be treated before the roof caves in.

Chapter 11

Paycheck to Paycheck

It is truly amazing how many people live from paycheck to paycheck. After working for years, I have met people who have no money in the bank and are overextended in credit card debt. Why do people live from paycheck to paycheck? How do people fail to save anything in the bank?

Placing Blame

One reason for this failure to save is based on the enlargement of the welfare state. If we lived in a society where there were no credit cards or entitlements, people would literally starve by living from paycheck to paycheck. When you live in that manner, you are looking for economic disaster, since one mishap will have a domino effect and knock the whole cart down. Children are no longer taught to save and parents don't think before they spend. How can you possibly live from paycheck to paycheck but spend $100 per month on cigarettes, and additional money for entertainment and alcohol? Unfortunately, if people had to rely more on themselves without assistance from government or credit cards, they would find a way.

Why were immigrants able to come to this land of ours with virtually nothing and able to save up for college to better their children and move out of ghettos? There is a spiritual crisis and feeling of hopelessness among a large segment of the population. People are not willing to sacrifice as did former generations. Since most of the World War II generation is now retired and our country is run by baby boomers, this mentality of expectation and instant gratification is ingrained in our society.

How dare I now work for $10 an hour when I was making $15 per hour? How dare I give up my new car, clothes and enjoyment? Life is such a drag that I need alcohol and entertainment. I'm not going to worry about the bills since I come first. I'm entitled to it, and the government should take care of me.

This mentality totally destroys the American Dream. The whole concept of the American Dream is OPPORTUNITY not EQUALITY. If you follow the Protestant work ethic of savings and working hard, you will not live from paycheck to paycheck. Also, if you live a moral lifestyle and stay out of trouble, you will have a much better opportunity to be able to save.

Years ago our parents didn't have the time to get in trouble because they spent too much time working, trying to provide for their families. Most Americans don't have the real drive to work hard when they are in the paycheck-to-paycheck mentality. How many people go back to school to better themselves or work a second job to save for their family? People spend too much time watching big screen TVs that they can't afford and playing video games on their financed computers instead of making an effort to better themselves.

But why put out all the effort when the government is there to come to your rescue? If you lose your job, you qualify for unemployment if you make a few calls a week. Why take a cut to $10 per hour when you were making $20 per hour? Unemployment will pay more. Some actually think that it is better for you to be on welfare rather than to accept the job paying minimum wage.

Develop Pride

People have to develop pride in working, saving and providing for their family. We have to instill the notion of working toward a goal, because if you have everything, what is there to look forward to? If you are driving a luxury vehicle when you're seventeen, how will you ever have the incentive to better yourself if you are given so much at a young age? In order to really appreciate good, you have to experience bad.

If you live on an island where the average family income is $50 per month, but you have never known anything else, you don't see this as bad. The poorest Americans live like kings compared to the rest of the world, but they always want more. If people just did their best, learned to live *within their means* and worked to improve their lot, they wouldn't be living from paycheck to paycheck.

Are You Planning to Fail?

One of the major causes of the paycheck-to-paycheck mentality is poor choices. People fail to plan. How can a married couple earning $80,000 per year have no savings and live from paycheck to paycheck? They are living above their means. Either they purchased a home where the mortgage payment is a substantial portion of their net income and/or they failed to anticipate all the costs of the new home or additional family commitments. These people had a solid income (even though the wife would later have children and not make her salary for a couple of years), so the mortgage company approved them immediately for a mortgage that constituted 35 percent of their net income. However, this couple never anticipated the cost of having children. When their first child was born the wife took off for two years to care for the child. To make up for her loss of income, the husband began running up the credit cards so he could continue to pay the mortgage and other necessities. Even when the wife resumed to full-time employment at a decent salary, bringing them back up to $80,000, they had additional costs of daycare, transportation and power lunches.

In seventeen years, I have seen this scenario happen so often because of people's failure to plan for these very common events. We are not talking about a major illness or injury. We are talking about a fact of life: women having children. If an illness or injury came into play, it would have the same devastating financial effect.

I am not talking about deprivation. I just advise people to cover all the bases by planning on contingencies. This is why you know better how much you can afford rather than what you are eligible to receive. The only thing that is constant in life is change. If you have a stellar job with a Fortune 500 company, there is no longer the paternalistic mentality by the company that you're family. You may keep on getting raises and more stature, or, one day the company may downsize. If you are self-employed, there may be more uncertainty. Even though this isn't the road to get rich quick, taking a conservative, planned approach can help you deal with life's curves.

The reason for paycheck-to-paycheck living is the choices that you've made. If you're a single mother who suddenly stopped getting child support, it was your choice that you went to bed with him. If you're paying child support, it was your choice to sleep with her. It is amazing that people can get intimate with somebody without knowing the person's physical, mental and emotional details. This is one reason why choices are so crucial.

Even though we all make mistakes, some mistakes linger for long periods of time and we pay for them dearly.

The other thing I hear is he's not the man I married. People have fundamental characteristics, but circumstances in their life create changes. When you make such an overwhelming decision to enter into a financial partnership with another party, you had better have a good idea of what you're getting into. If you enjoy the jet-set lifestyle and your significant other is a homebody, you will not only have social problems but there will be a financial impact. On the other hand, if you live a very simple life and the significant other spends freely, this will cause social and financial problems. I agree with noted psychologists, who state that if couples were all alike they would be bored out of their minds; however, a successful relationship must have three common denominators: 1) religious, 2) political, and 3) economic. Without these basic bonds there are too many chances for a blowup. To sustain a marriage or another significant relationship takes a lot of work, effort and planning. If you are not always a step ahead in the chess game of life, then you will never be prepared.

Finally

There are no guarantees in life; however, inadequate preparation will lead to an existence of living from paycheck to paycheck with no safety net to deal with life's challenges. Keep in mind the following points:

- The welfare state takes away responsibility on the individual to save, due to all the entitlements.
- The American Dream stands for OPPORTUNITY NOT EQUALITY.
- People don't have the incentive to take a lesser-paying job

when the government provides entitlements.

- People fail to plan for life's natural occurrences, such as child-birth.

- To have a successful relationship, the couple must have three common denominators:

    1. Religion,
    2. Politics, and
    3. Economics.

Chapter 12

Are Two Incomes Really Necessary?

One of the biggest reasons for financial turmoil is due to one spouse's loss of income. It seems that people always want more and more, assuming that things will always stay the same. Life is not a straight highway, and people fail to realize that there are always bumps and curves along the way. People don't understand that a lot of times the "extra" pay stub has a serious detrimental effect. What is the real cost? First, people feel that, because there is extra income, they can afford a more expensive home, a new car or more expensive "work" clothes, and if there are young children, this also means additional childcare costs. If you figure out what you are really taking home with the "extra" paycheck, does it justify the extra wants and desires?

When you start looking for homes, both brokers and mortgage companies will tell you that you are eligible for a substantial mortgage. Without being cynical, the larger the mortgage the more income the mortgage company earns. Also, the real estate broker doesn't worry about whether you can afford the home since he is getting a larger commission. It is unfortunate that so few lenders seek to really serve homebuyers. I feel that some brokers are really concerned that you live in a good neighborhood. However, monetary issues should be totally within your control. Also, brokers and mortgage companies look at only a pay stub because it gives them concrete evidence of income. Ironically, a self-employed person who earns substantially more than the person on the "fixed income" will have a much harder time being approved for the mortgage. When you are looking for a home, don't let others convince you that you can afford something when you feel uncomfortable.

The Consequences of a Second Income

Unfortunately, we presently live in a different time than when our parents grew up. People no longer stay at the same job for years with all of today's layoffs and downsizing. Thus, it is still my opinion that you should only base *one* spouse's income in determining what type of house you can afford.

> *If you look at that second paycheck, how much Net income does it really mean to you?*

Remember, this can propel you into a higher tax bracket, plus you have to think of FICA, state and disability payments. If you have young children, how much of that money will have to go to a childcare provider, which gives you a minimum tax benefit? Certain types of employment require specific clothes, which means that more money out of the second paycheck will be spent. A new car may be desired because many people assume that a used vehicle won't get them to work, especially if there is a long commute. This also results in larger fuel and auto maintenance costs.

Remember, this one additional paycheck results in numerous additional expenses, with no tax benefits, that are never taken into account when determining how much you can afford if you are looking for a home. It may be difficult to live on one paycheck, but look at the social as well as economic issues.

Isn't it your responsibility to bring up your own children rather than have a third party take care of your children?

When you decided to have your children, didn't you realize that your parenting responsibility came first?

However, does the second paycheck really make your life better when you consider all the costs involved? When you consider all the expenses, without tax deductions, involved, the economic benefits rarely outweigh the costs. Only if the two incomes are utilized in a proper manner to accumulate net worth for the family rather than the possession of material needs should families consider whether two paychecks are necessary.

Growing up I had several friends whose families only had one wage earner. They never went without food, clothing or shelter and they all got college degrees. These friends' parents understood the notion of sacrifice for their children, and just had different priorities than the current instantaneous gratification generation.

It Can Be Done — This Is Your Choice

Statistics show that most families in the 1990s "needed" both parents to work to maintain their life style. As a result of both parents working, childcare expenses became a necessity. It has been estimated that the cost of raising one child up until age 17 can range from $151,170 to $293,400, depending on whether you qualify as a low-income family, earning under $29,000 per annum, to a high-income family, earning over $48,300 per annum.[1]

If you have children and wish to work, childcare has to be paid either via a daycare center, baby-sitter, nanny, relative or au pair. The costs of individual care for nannies or baby-sitters can be substantial and range from $200-400 per week, plus, you are responsible for 7.65 percent in Social Security taxes, plus unemployment insurance equal to .008 percent of the first $7,000, plus state unemployment insurance equal to 2.5 percent of the first $7,000.[2] Daycare costs can also be substantial, running from $50 to $125 per week.[3] Finally, some people drop their children off with other parents who provide care for a group of children. This may be the lowest cost, but there may be an issue of quality and the ratio of children to the caregiver.[4]

After raising young children, there is the question of college tuition. These costs must be anticipated since college expenses are increasing at an exponential rate. Recent projections can project the cost of a public college from $8,985 per year starting in the year 2000 to $17,056 by 2011. In contrast, private schools can run from $23,985 in 2000 to $45,531 in 2011.[5]

The Boomer Factor

Since we are now a generation of baby boomers; (76 million people born between 1946 and 1964)[6], it is important to examine the noneconomic factors that have affected us. Unlike their parents and grandparents, boomers chose to move out at a younger age, which put a debt in their income since they had to support themselves.[7] Secondly, incomes have not grown as fast to keep up with expenses as in the past. In their parents' generation, income increased 529 percent between the ages of 20-30, while baby boomers income only increased 34 percent during that same period.[8] However, the major issue between boomers and their parents is that boomers are competing for fewer jobs with the added responsibility of saving for college for their kids and caring for their elder parents. This creates a financial crunch.[9]

Similarly, in the nineties a lot of previous assumptions about employment were questioned. There used to be a notion that employers would care for their employees during hard times, and if you did well you would be with the same employer for life. Now the rules of the game have changed. Instead of an employer–employee relationship, it appears that most employment scenarios consist of a project scenario. An employee is similar to a free agent on a sports team.[10] Similarly, entrepreneurs may not be able to rely on their past successes in a changing global environment.

Thus, in the overall scheme is the second income really a benefit? Compared to our parent's generation, the increase in income from your twenties to thirties has decreased substantially. When you consider all the non-tax-deductible expenses, such as childcare, transportation costs, auto maintenance, health insurance plus the high taxes for federal, state, Social Security and disability insurance, does the second income make sense financially?

The biggest myth is that it is a necessity that both spouses must work.

However, the issue comes to spending. With respect to baby boomers and generation Xers, many have no conception of budgeting since they have never had to sacrifice as our parents did during the First World War, Depression and Second World War.

More Proof in the Pudding

I have examined over five thousand people's monthly expenses, and they either overspend and know it or have no conception how much money is going out each month, which results in a financial nightmare. I have met families of five who claim their monthly grocery bill is $300 and monthly clothing bill is

$50. However, besides not having any understanding of how much they spend, people fail to put aside money for emergencies. Also, many families view spending as a social activity. Unfortunately, many people are not good spenders. People purchase high-ticket incomes without realizing how much the loan is actually going to cost. People finance automobiles, furniture, appliances — and anything else under the sun — at interest rates over 20 percent.

To control spending you must examine your expenses over the last year at a minimum, otherwise, when a major bill comes, it will have a snowball effect and set you behind. You must write down everything you spend and charge, being sure to include all the ATM and debit transactions to see exactly where your money is going.

Without actually examining your monthly expenses, you will never know how much you can afford for an auto, mortgage or rent payment.

In addition, most people let themselves be sold rather than thoroughly planning their purchases. The advertising folks impress upon us the need for new products. Sometimes it doesn't make sense to repair an old item when the cost of repair is extremely high. Even with the marketing and advertising, which floods the market, many people never do their homework before purchasing an item. I would advise you to check out *Consumer Reports* since it scrutinizes all types of consumer products and gives you independent recommendations.

Finally

You should always comparison shop or haggle with the dealer. So many people are overly concerned about getting approved that they don't consider all the legal implications. Before they know it they are bound to one-sided contracts. If people change the way they spend and shop, there won't be that urgent need to have two incomes. Sure, there may be sacrifices, but in the long run it will teach you a lesson on controlling your spending to avoid the debt trap.

Keep the following points in mind:

- A second paycheck may not make economic sense when you consider all of the tax implications and additional expenses, many of which have no tax benefit.
- The costs of raising children affect your budget, and you must plan for it.
- Incomes have not grown as fast in recent times as they did in our parents' times.
- Baby boomers have the twofold obligation of caring for their children and elderly parents at the same time.
- People should plan their purchases and negotiate. Don't get caught paying outrageous interest rates on high-ticket items that you cannot afford.

Chapter 13

Home Equity and Other Killer Loans

If you are a homeowner, you are constantly barraged with ads about saving money by using the equity in your home to pay off credit card debts and for home improvements, college tuition, a vacation or anything else your heart desires. The biggest threat to you, and one of the biggest profits for the bank, is the home equity loan. These are always bad deals because you bet your home against your ability to satisfy the debt.

Is It Worth the Risk?

I see so many people who, due to financial mismanagement, get a home equity loan to satisfy credit card debt. Because they haven't dealt with the symptom that caused the debt, they will soon find themselves with new credit card debt in addition to an additional mortgage on their real estate. You always hear on TV and the radio that the loan may be tax deductible. However, in many cases interest on these home equity loans may not always be a tax deduction if the home equity loan line of credit is greater than the amount you paid for your home or it's not a purchase money mortgage.[1]

Even if the loan is tax deductible, is it worth using your home as collateral?

Let's examine the real-life scenario of a couple who got behind on credit cards while the wife was out on maternity leave. If you take a second mortgage, the bank can foreclose on your home; however, the credit card company has to sue you to get a judgment. You must be careful because many credit cards for second mortgages look like ordinary credit cards, but the difference is incredible (i.e., your home is at risk if you default).

Many people I have met over the last 17 years think the answer to all their problems is to refinance or get a quick fix since it doesn't deal with the reasons why you got into the debt trap. This is analogous to treating a chronic illness with prescriptions while missing the underlying reason for the illness. Secondly, banks and finance companies are going to consider people in debt as a high risk.

If you have no financial problems or refinance your mortgage because interest rates have declined, then more power to you.

However, if you are in deep debt and have credit problems, you are not a candidate to get a great deal, because you are high risk. Normally, this will come in the form of a high interest rate plus substantial points at closing.

There are several dangers associated with these home equity loans:

- First, many home equity loans require balloon payments. This means that if you have stayed current throughout the length of your loan, you may owe a large balloon payment at the end of the loan if you're not fortunate enough to be able to refinance the balloon.

- Second, you must be wary of variable interest rates. For example, some mortgages have no limit on how high the interest rates can go.

- Third, points may be charged on the entire amount of the line of credit, even if you borrow only a small fraction of the line of credit. If you have $100,000 line of credit and you have to pay 4 points that constitutes $4,000, if you borrow only $16,000 you are paying back $20,000 or 25 percent interest.

- Fourth, be careful of the home equity loan checks. Believe me, nobody is giving you money for free. These are cons for secured mortgages for which you put your home on the line.

Remember, when you have a financial problem, you become a high risk. Banks aren't going to give you money because they feel sorry for you or they are your buddies. Banks make huge profits and your home will be at stake. Unfortunately, many people don't even realize they have put their home up as collateral until it is too late.[2]

More Bad-Idea Loans

The second trap is the consolidation loan. These come in two types: secured and unsecured. Secured loans are non-possessory, non-purchase money security interests. This means that when you ask a company for $5,000, they will ask you to list all the personal property that you own such as a car, appliances, sports equipment or any other similar personal property. What this means is that you have given the bank a security interest in all the personal property that you listed. If you don't make payments, they can repossess the collateral that you pledged. This is in addition to the astronomical interest rate you will be charged for being high risk. Again, these loan companies are not your pals. They know that you are desperate for a loan, and they are making a huge profit because you are a high risk. These loans are not even a short-term fix since you are paying back an unreasonable amount *and* pledging your personal property as collateral if you default.

There are also unsecured personal loans from finance companies. These loans are not any better than the non-possessory, non-purchase money security interests, except that you have not pledged any personal property as collateral. However, you are still paying an outrageous interest rate because you became a high-risk borrower once you defaulted.

Finally

I can't emphasize enough that another loan *is not the answer* to debt because you are only replacing one debt with a new debt. The answer is learning to budget. Without a sound spending plan, you will fall behind on all future home equity loans or personal loans that were used as a quick-fix solution.

Keep the following points in mind when considering loans:

- When you take a home equity loan, you bet your home against your ability to satisfy the debt.

- Not all home equity loans are tax deductible. Check with your accountant or the IRS.

- Be careful of potential traps with home equity loans.

- Many consolidation loans are secured, which means the lending agencies can repossess your property if you don't satisfy the loan. Also, the interest rate on these loans is astronomical.

- Loans are not the answer to debt because they treat only the symptom rather than the cause.

- There are no quick-fix solutions to debt.

Chapter 14

Starting Your Own Business

This chapter serves as only a synopsis for starting your own business for an individual and trying to protect yourself from debt. There are numerous books which go into depth about the intricacies of a business plan and starting a business.

Your Piece of the Pie

The American Dream is to work for yourself and to have your own business. Thousands have made their fortunes. Unfortunately, we rarely hear about the people who have failed because of poor economic planning.

Many people incorporate because a corporation has limited liability. This means that if the corporation has assets of $10,000, the most the shareholder can be held responsible for are the corporate assets. However, if you incorporate and create a separate legal entity, you must comply with all the formalities of the corporation, or creditors can try to "pierce the corporate veil" and go after you individually.

In my years of practice I have seen several individuals create their own financial dilemmas by incorporating and signing a personal guarantee using their home or other assets. This destroys the whole purpose of incorporating, which is to create limited liability.

Insurance Is Necessary

Probably one of the most underestimated necessities for any business is insurance. The most important insurance for a professional is malpractice insurance. In such a litigious society, everyone is going to be sued no matter how diligent they are in pursuing their professional endeavors. Any other business needs liability insurance. Under the liberal interpretations taken by courts, businesses have been held responsible under the doctrine of foreseeability. If a businessman is hit with a substantial judgment without the proper amount of liability insurance, this could lead to financial ruin.

Health Insurance

People don't realize how important good health insurance is. One of the most unexpected problems in life is unforeseen medical problems. In light of the fact that so many Americans are overweight, they are at a very high risk for high blood pressure, stroke, diabetes and other debilitating illnesses. The costs for medical treatment and hospitalizations have been skyrocketing.

In 1990, I was hospitalized for a few days and got a bill for over $5,000. For a more serious hospitalization, bills could run up in the thousands and thousands of dollars and wipe out your lifetime of savings.

Disability Insurance

In many small businesses, the owner is the life and blood of the business; and without the owner's labor, there would be substantial losses to the business. Therefore, it is imperative for the owner of the business to have substantial disability insurance to cover his normal monthly expenses plus business expenses. Disability insurance is imperative for a self-employed owner to survive in the case of injury or illness. Remember, life is full of uncertainties, so you have to investigate every conceivable method to protect your family and business from financial ruin.

Workers Compensation Insurance

Under the laws of my state (NJ), it may be a criminal offense not to have workers compensation insurance, since injured employees are entitled medical treatment, temporary disability and permanent disability, if applicable. This is a requirement that is mandated if you have employees, and failure to provide it can lead to serious monetary losses and possible criminal prosecution under the law.

Hazard and Property Insurance

Whether you own a business or home, it is imperative that you have hazard or property insurance to protect the equipment and inventory of the business in case of fire, theft or act of God. I would speak to a reputable agent to protect yourself against any unforeseen damage. It is true that insurance costs money, but if it is an ordinary and necessary expense of doing business, then it is a business expense under section 162 of the Internal Revenue Code.

Choose a Business Type

Now that you have your insurance lined up, the next step is to decide what type of business entity you are forming. Three basic entities are: the sole proprietor, the partnership or the corporation. A sole proprietor is the simplest legal form. However, you still have regular tax obligations, which would be more costly for a partnership or corporation. However, the biggest problem with a sole proprietorship is that you set yourself up for unlimited liability. So you need to have adequate liability insurance to protect your property from being seized by a creditor.

A partnership is another legal entity to consider. However, you may be liable for your partner's mistakes if he makes any. If you are entering a partnership, make sure you have competent legal counsel to draft or review the partnership agreement to adequately protect your interest.

A corporation gives you limited liability as long as you comply with all the corporate requirements and don't personally guarantee any contracts that would endanger you personally.

Capital

The best way to start a business is to set aside a certain amount of money for a business. But the expenses for payroll, rent, costs, business equipment, insurance, advertising, postage, duplicates, publications, accounting, phone, seminars and entertainment expenses can be substantial. In addition, you need an office, computer, copier, fax machine, typewriters, bookkeeper, copy paper, stationery, and the items necessary to keeping the equipment working.

If you have a great idea and don't have the capital, one idea is to get venture capitalists to fund you, and you give them a percentage of the profits, to avoid borrowing a substantial amount of money that would put you in debt. I have seen too many people lose their homes by taking large home equity loans to fund their businesses, without realizing the competitive nature of the business.

One very good idea for professionals is a *space for service* arrangement. A space for service arrangement is where you rent space and, instead of paying rent, provide services in exchange. For example, if you are a young attorney and need office space at $600 per month, you would make an arrangement with the other attorney/landlord that you would provide 20 hours of services in exchange for use of the space. (You are charging $30 per hour to the other lawyer.) This saves the other lawyer from hiring an associate to handle conflicts and research.

A space for service arrangement would save you money on rent, copying machine, fax machine, etc. It is only a temporary arrangement, but it will give you a start without your incurring substantial debt. You have to expect to lose money in your own business during the first year; but after gradually developing a clientele and referral base, your business should gradually expand and you can incrementally increase your marketing.

I feel that it is too much of a risk to throw thousands of dollars into marketing initially. Unfortunately, when you are in business, you can never let sleeping dogs lay. There will always be competitors trying to cut into your market share.

Customers

There is no guarantee for satisfying customers, although the customer should always come first. Remember, every customer is a potential referrer of new customers. If you don't treat customers properly, you will lose them. Surveys have shown, unfortunately, that negative assessments of a company spread a lot quicker than positive feedback. Customers want you to take a personal interest in them. Even though price is very important, customers want full value; they want availability, choice, quality and service. If you don't provide the quality service, it will eventually hurt you.

In any business, one of your most important assets is your customer list. This list is invaluable to you. A general rule of thumb is that you should stay in touch with your customers by sending mailings to them at least on a quarterly basis so your name stays in the customer's head.

Besides weekly necessities, several businesses aren't in need until a situation occurs. You can be the greatest plumber in the world but unless a customer has a plumbing problem, your services won't be necessary. If you get over the hurdles of covering the ordinary expenses without exposing yourself personally to a financial ruin, you have an opportunity to create more financial freedom to stay out of debt.

Finally

When considering starting your own business, keep the following points in mind:

- Know the different types of legal entities available before starting a business. Talk to a CPA to go over all of the tax implications.

- You must get liability insurance or malpractice insurance to protect you against a large judgment. If you have any kind of business establishment, anyone can sue you for an injury. As stated earlier, any professional can be sued for malpractice with all the litigation in our society. If you don't have malpractice insurance, you are setting yourself up, since no matter how careful you are, you are setting yourself up for trouble.

  Also, if you don't have disability insurance, you can have a substantial loss of income if you're out of work for an illness or disability.

  Finally, without health insurance, medical bills can lead to financial ruin.

- Be careful about taking a home equity loan to provide capital for your business. If you can't raise the capital, try to get venture capitalists to share in the profits in exchange for their capital.

- Generate a customer list and send quarterly mailings to build a clientele.

Chapter 15

The Tax Man

Three of the most feared letters in the English language are I-R-S.

Many people I come into contact with owe money to the IRS because they failed to pay income taxes, employment taxes (941), or FUTA taxes (940), or have personal responsibility taxes from a corporation that has failed.

You Can Run, But You Can't Hide

The IRS has tremendous power because, unlike other creditors, they can levy on property without court authorization. I have had clients who have had almost their entire paycheck or bank account seized due to money they owe the IRS. Once the IRS is in gear, you may be forced into bankruptcy to stop this unbridled power, unless you have already worked out a payment plan with the Internal Revenue Service.

I can tell you from personal experience that if you don't anticipate tax liability, you may owe a large sum of money that was unexpected. The first thing you have to do is work out with your CPA an estimated tax schedule. These payments must be made on April 15, June 15, September 15 and January 15. It is imperative that you set aside money each *week* toward your tax liability. The worst possible thing is to anticipate money coming in without having a plan. Even if you have a small business, you must put aside a certain amount of money each week so you can afford your estimated taxes. If you wait to pay taxes at the end of the year, you may be responsible for penalties. It is thus advisable to have a set schedule so you can learn to deal with the slow and busy times when you are self-employed.

The other major tax that you must be prepared for is 941 taxes. Each week, or every other week, depending on payroll, you must make sure you set aside money for 941 taxes that you take out of your employee's pay. The general rule of thumb is that if you take out 7.65 percent of your employee's wages for FICA, you owe the IRS two times the FICA plus the federal tax. Depending on your type of business, this money has to be paid to the IRS either by bank deposits or direct payments to the IRS.

Finally, you must set aside money for state taxes and disability taxes. Unfortunately, this is a very difficult endeavor for many because your tax payments are based on how much you earned the preceding year with regard to estimated taxes.

Save, Save and Save Again

If you don't plan for taxes, you are headed for serious problems. This goes back to the whole notion of saving for a rainy day and forcing you to put money away for taxes. In the order of priority, after your mortgage, you must meet your tax obligation, otherwise the IRS can take a lien on your home or wipe out your bank accounts and other assets. If you are fortunate, you can do an offer and compromise and work out a payment plan.

Please be careful even if you are incorporated. If you have major control over a corporation, you may *individually* be responsible for corporate taxes under the concept of personal responsibility. I had one client who was under the impression that she owed the state taxing authority around $15,000. Her corporation tried to reorganize but was unsuccessful and then liquidated.

Because of the concept of personal responsibility, since she and her husband were the driving force behind the corporation, they were personally responsible for over $50,000 to the State Taxing Authority.

Finally

In our country you are presumed innocent until proven guilty. This is not the way it works with the Internal Revenue Service. If you don't have an excellent journal and receipts for certain deductions, you will not only owe the money, but you will be assessed interest and penalties. The system makes it hard enough, so allocate your payments and keep good records and a journal in case of an audit.

When considering taxes, keep in mind the following points:

- Set aside money on a weekly basis for the tax man for estimated taxes. If you wait until the end of the year, you may not have the funds or you may be hit with penalties.

- Set aside money for payroll taxes each week and for state taxes each month.

- Keep excellent records. They will help to protect you if you're ever audited.

Chapter 16

The New Debt Trap

After World War II, the GI Bill was supposed to give everyone an opportunity to improve his or her life by getting a college or graduate school degree. Unfortunately, many persons today get into incredible debt by trying to better themselves, and student loans have to be viewed as any other type of obligation.

Schools, like any other product, try to sell their services, and students have to use discretion in obtaining student loans. Like any other debt, student loans should be taken out with caution because they become large obligations that may take years to pay back.

You have to realize that, if you go to an extremely expensive undergraduate institution, you have to measure the true value of the institution with the projected benefit to you in the real world. Before you decide to take out large student loans, you should take a careful look at the educational institutions and their records.

If a student loan will create a large amount of debt, you may consider working part time and going to school part time so that you can save for school. There is no rush to finish school immediately because, once you graduate, you are going to be working for the rest of your life. It is very difficult when you are young; however, if you are setting yourself up for $100,000 in student loans, it may lead to serious debt problems down the line.

I've met several ex-medical students who never graduated and are stuck with substantial student loans without any relief. I'm not saying that you shouldn't go to an expensive graduate school, but you must think in advance. Ask yourself if what you are doing today is what you planned to do 10 years ago. What happens if you get burned out in a given profession and are unable to pay those loans? You must do your homework and really research the school and the cost involved. This is your first responsibility as a student in the real world.

Also, remember that those future student loan payments, which you have no concern for at this time, may have a serious impact in your budget down the line. Is there truly any difference in your future employment picture whether you go to an expensive undergraduate institution compared to a less expensive state school? After considering the evidence you must carefully decide how much in student loans is worth the future debt! Before you get involved with establishing budgets in the real world, carefully assess the costs and keep the following points in mind:

- Be careful about the undergraduate or graduate school you choose because the student loan payments may strangle you for years.

- Be sure to research the school's reputation and job placement.

Chapter 17

Does Character Matter?

As stated in the introduction, some people fall into debt because of circumstances that are out of their control: a serious accident that put you out of work; a debilitating illness that caused medical bills that were not covered by insurance; or you were a victim of a crime and lost substantial assets. However, many people fall into debt because of mistakes that they make that are totally within their control.

It's Entirely Up to You

All of us have free will and are totally responsible for all the choices we have made. Whatever you're doing today is based on choices you made or didn't make over the course of your life.

Many people laugh at the notion of abstinence or safe sex.

For many young people, sex is a game where they keep score. However, both parties don't seem to realize that NO method of birth control is 100 percent certain. Also, without the notion of family and wanting that child to be nurtured in a warm, loving family, there is a strong likelihood that the relationship will fall apart. However, besides the relationship between the unmarried persons falling apart, there is a financial impact on both parties. Evidence shows that there is a much greater chance that a single female parent will end up in bankruptcy than a married couple, since the one parent has both responsibilities and will really find trouble if child support never starts or is cut off.[1] On the other side of the coin, I have seen numerous clients who can never turn their financial picture around because they have child support obligations that don't go away.

Character Matters in Marriage

Those partners with whom you establish relationships will have a major impact on your financial future. I am not a psychologist and don't understand why marriages fall apart; however, too many people lack a strong foundation. From personal experience, I can tell you that it is essential that three common bonds exist: economic, religious and political. Also, without trust and communication there is a greater likelihood that a marriage will fail.

Is it not surprising that, with one out of every two marriages ending in divorce, there is an emotional and financial toll? As a result of the emotional toll, there are incredible financial costs; spouses need continued counseling in certain cases after bitter, contested divorce battles. Children suffer irreparable damage. No party is ever the winner. Finally, the parties suffer incredible financial debt since it doesn't take a rocket scientist to understand that it is more expensive to run two households than one.

I am not saying that people should never divorce. When there is abuse that threatens the health, education and welfare of the parties, you cannot risk your physical or emotional health when one spouse won't change. Unfortunately, many marriages terminate only because the parties didn't want to work on the marriage.

The whole notion of "until death do us part" has itself parted by the wayside.

If people leave a marriage for reasons other than extreme abuse or adultery, then they are just giving in to instantaneous gratification.

In New Jersey, a person can get divorced under mental cruelty if under one's subjective view "it is unreasonable for one to continue residing with the other and it effects their health and welfare."[2] In an article in the *New Jersey Law Journal* written several years ago, the author determined that in the best of marriages, one can always find a handful of instances of "mental cruelty" to qualify for divorce.

My response is that marriage is not a joke or something to do because all your friends are doing it. Your spouse should be your best friend and someone you can fully trust. A strong marriage is not a guarantee against debt; but a divorce will give you a much better chance of unwanted financial debt and emotional baggage.

Remember that, in our society, the media sells instantaneous gratification and there are no limits. There are no limits for you as individuals, but buying that car, house or other material goods that you cannot afford is not unlimited power – this can create unlimited debt.

Ignore the Joneses

You need to have enough character not to worry about whether other people approve. Does it really bother you that you are debt free and drive a 10-year-old car when your neighbor is leasing a spanking new luxury vehicle? Can you deal with the fact that some neighborhood kids can tease your kids because their clothes aren't designer brand? Can you accept taking a modest vacation while your coworker puts a few thousand dollars on his credit card to take a luxury vacation? Do you feel upset while your neighbor purchased new construction and your home is over 30 years old?

Contrary to the myth that you are *entitled* to have anything or everything, you have to realize that to truly appreciate what you have, you have to earn it. You are entitled to be the best you are physically, socially, spiritually and financially, but not at the expense of debt.

If you fail to plan and just accumulate material goods without earning them, one day you will have to pay for them.

It takes a very strong, self-confident person to take personal responsibility and understand the meaning of sacrifice when you have a family.

Do you need a home that has enough rooms for every child if you have a mortgage that is half of your net income, or do you want a small home with a low mortgage that is secure?

What Would You Do?

It may seem hard to believe, but when our ancestors came to this country a few families lived in the same house. Several people shared beds, a toilet, bathroom, and there was no air conditioning or TVs, but people survived. Now people need not only a TV and VCR in every room, but they need a big screen TV. People who don't have enough money to pay their normal bills charge entertainment centers, big screen TVs and finance fully loaded cars that cost almost as much as their mortgage payments.

Unfortunately, people expect to have all the amenities without budgeting for or earning their material possessions. We live in a society where honor, duty and morality are mocked, since our role models in sports and politics set such poor examples.

Americans now expect that Big Brother should come into play when they fail to take personal responsibility. If suddenly people had no safety net to fall back upon, then there would be a lot more people who would take personal responsibility for their actions.

If student loans were eliminated, people would force themselves to save something for their children's college or the children would work part time and put themselves through school. If Social Security were eliminated, people would be forced to save during their lives so they wouldn't be destitute when they reached retirement.

Only when people learn to rely on themselves and plan for the future will they live debt free. There must be a different mentality than purely living for today without concern at all for tomorrow.

Recognize the Mistakes of the Past

There must be balance: people may not have to live like hermits in sacrifice, but our country has gone the other way where nobody wants to sacrifice or take any responsibility for their financial sanity. This all started with the sixties and the whole notion of counterculture. Many hit songs out of the 1960s symbolize this notion of instant gratification without concern for anybody but me. But, with that counterculture of the sixties, the "me" generation of the seventies and the "greed" generation of the eighties, people have lost a lot of the values of the World War II generation.

With the rise of unprecedented prosperity in the fifties and sixties, people lost the will to take charge of their lives. Ironically as more prosperity emerged, the "War on Poverty" created an underclass of people who relied more on government. However, this emergence of individual rights in the sixties resulted in entitlement to anything. Soon, creditors expanded their marketing by offering more and more credit. However, people lost the old notions of thrift, savings and hard work and wanted things yesterday.

My premise is that you don't have to be part of the masses that are leveraged to the hilt. What are we teaching our children if we just accumulate material goods without saving, earning or working toward it? Our economy is so fueled by credit. Americans have to get back to basics if we are ever going to get out of this mess of 5.8 trillion dollars in consumer debt.

Ask Yourself

It all begins with character. Am I really better off than my parents when I have minimal money in the bank and have no equity in anything I own? How can I feel secure when the bank owns my furniture, my car and my house? Is it worth it to keep up with the Joneses when I'm working constantly to keep up with my payments? Are all the material possessions really making me happy?

This is not an easy proposition because you have to make a lot of sacrifices. You can do it. If you really go over your budget and figure out what is within your ability to pay, you will be a lot happier.

Happiness is not found through material wealth, and jealousy will never lead you to anything but stress in your life.

Even though certain things are not within our control, we have more control over things than we realize. We all have free will and have control over our choices. We chose our friends, our jobs, our lovers, our homes and our cars. If we constantly want more, the debt trap will get us. If we live a life of honor, sacrifice, and traditional values, it will be the first step in avoiding the debt trap.

It's your choice.

Keep in mind the following points when considering the importance of character:

- Who you choose to have a relationship with will have a definite impact on your financial future.
- Divorce creates an emotional and financial toll.
- Marriage is a commitment that should not be taken lightly.
- You have to earn your material possessions.
- If there were no safety net to fall back on, people would take more personal responsibility for their actions.
- Only when you learn to rely on yourself and plan for the future will you live debt free.
- Only a life of honor, sacrifice and traditional values will help you avoid the debt trap.

End Notes

Chapter 1

1. *Surviving the Squeeze,* Stephen M. Pollan and Mark Levine, Collier Books, McMillan Publishing Company, 1994, p. 170-171.

2. *Consumer Bankruptcy News*, Sept. 5, 2002, Volume 12, Issue 12, p. 1.

3. http://www.bloombeg.com/money/loan/mtge-calc.html

Chapter 2

1. http://www.divorceinfo.com/bknywomenfiling.htm

2. *Consumer Bankruptcy Report*, August 26, 1999, Volume 9, Issue 1, p. 1.

3. *Ibid*

4. *Ibid*, at p. 12

5. *Ibid*

6. *Information Plus – The Social welfare*, Wylie Texas 75098-7006. 1998 Edition, p. 23.

7. *Information Plus – The American Family*, Wylie Texas 75098-7006, 1999 Edition, p. 2.

8. *Ibid*

9. US Dept of Labor Bureau of Labor Statistics, *Handbook of Labor Sta-*

tistics, 1989, *Employment and Earnings,* January 1998, and unpublished tables, *See Information Plus – The American Family,* Wylie, Texas 57098-7006, p. 91.

10. *Information Plus – Social welfare*, Wylie, Texas 75098-7006, p. 45.

11. *Information Plus – The American Family*, Wylie, Texas 75098-7006, 1999 Edition, p. 37.

12. http://www.ssa.gov/history/history6.html.

13. *Information Plus – Social welfare*, Wylie, Texas 75098-7006, p. 4.

14. *Ibid,* at p. 6

15. *Ibid*

Chapter 4

1. 38I US 479 (1965)

2. 410 US 113 (1973)

3. *Faith or Fear,* Elliott Abrams, The Free Press. New York 1997, pp. 99-101.

4. *Ibid*, at p. 102

5. *Ibid*, at p. 103

Chapter 5

1. *Consumer Bankruptcy News*, Volume 8, Issue 15, April 22 1999, p. 2.

2. *The Law & Legislation of Credit cards*, Irving J. Stone, London, Ocean Publication 1987, p. 2.

3. *Expressing America: A Critique of the Global Credit card Society*, George Ritzer, Pine Forge Press, 1995, p. 31.

4. *Ibid*, at p. 14

5. *Ibid*, at p. 15

6. *Ibid*, at p. 13

7. James Poniewozit, "Today I am a man; Charge it", *Fortune Magazine*, Dec. 21, 1998, p. 44.

8. *Ibid,* at p. 48

9. *Expressing America: A Critique of the Global Credit card Society,* George Ritzer, Pine Forge Press, 1995, p. 14.

10. *Ibid,* at p. 31

11. *Ibid,* at p. 2

12. *Ibid,* at p. 3

13. *Ibid,* at p. 5

14. *Ibid,* at p. 6

15. *Ibid,* at p. 46-47

16. Janice Castro, *Charge it Your Way,* Time, July 1, 1991, pp. 50-51

17. Albert B. Crenshaw, "Taking Credit For a Card Using Boom", *Washington Post*, Oct. 17, 1993, pages 1 and 3.

18. *American Bankers Association Bank Card Fact Book*, Washington, DC: American Bankers Association, 1990, p. 9

19. Michael T. Killian, *Personal Credit US Credit cards, They're Just Like Drugs Personal Credit*, (US) 6/15/97. Retrieved October 1, 1999 from the World wide web:
http:/…/aa061597.htm?if=ma+cob==home+tmag=3549925230417 +mint=3549925283041.

20. *Ibid.*

21. U.S. Census Bureau Statistical Abstract of the U.S.: 2001, 121st Edition. Washington, DC, 2001, Library of Congress, Card No. 4-18089, p. 727.

22. *Consumers in Trouble, A Study of Debtors in Default*, David Caplovitz, Free Press, 1974, pps. 1&2.

23. *Consumer Bankruptcy News*, March 25, 1999, Volume 8, Issue 13, p. 1

24. *Consumer Bankruptcy News*, Sept. 5, 2002, Volume 12, Issue 2, p. 1.

25. *Consumers in Trouble, A Study of Debtors in Default*, David Caplovitz, Free Press, 1974, pps. 2-3.

26. *Ibid,* at p. 51

27. *Ibid,* at p. 57

28. *Ibid*

29. *What Every Credit card User Needs to Know*, Howard Strong, Henry Holt and Company, New York. 1999, pps. 26-27.

30. *Expressing America, A Critique of the Global Credit card Society*, George Ritzer, Pine Forge Press, London 1995, pps. 4-5.

31. *What every Credit card User Needs to Know*, Howard Strong, Henry Holt and Company, New York, 1999, pps. 27-28.

32. *Ibid,* at p. 30

33. *Ibid,* at p. 33

34. Andrew Tobias, "Beware the Plastic Loan Shark", Time, Jan. 10, 1994, p. 20.

35. *Expressing America: A critique of the Global Credit card Society*, George Ritzer, Pine Forge Press London 1995, pp. 72-73.

Chapter 6

1. Anthony Robbins, *Personal Power II: The Driving Force, Volume 7, How to Unleash the Financial Genius Within You*, Robbins Research International, Inc. San Diego, CA 1993,1996.

2. *Ibid*

Chapter 9

1. *The Millionaire Next Door*, Thomas J. Stanley, William D. Danko, Longstreet Press, Marietta, GA 1996, p. 37.

Chapter 12

1. *Surviving the Squeeze,* Stephen M. Pollan and Mark Levine, Collier Books, Macmillan Publishing Company, 1994, pp. 170-171.

2. *Ibid,* at p. 175

3. *Ibid,* at p. 176

4. *Ibid,* at p. 177

5. *Ibid,* at p. 193

6. *Ibid,* at p. 1

7. *Ibid,* at p. 9

8. *Ibid,* at p. 10

9. *Ibid,* at p. 14

10. *Ibid*, at p. 43

Chapter 13

1. *What Every Credit card User Needs to Know,* Howard Strong, Henry Holt and Company, New York, 1999, p. 63

2. *Ibid,* at p. 65

Chapter 17

1. *Consumer Bankruptcy News*, August 26, 1999, Volume 9, Issue 1, pp. 12-13.

2. *NJSA* 2A: 34-2(c)

Suggested Reading

Consumers in Trouble, a Study of Debtors in Default, David Caplovitz, Free Press, 1974.

The Courage to Be Rich, Suze Ormon, Riverhead Books, A Member of Penguin Putnam, Inc., New York, 1999.

Expressing America: A Critique of the Global Credit card Society, George Ritzer, Pine Forge Press, 1998.

Faith or Fear, Elliott Abrams, The Free Press, New York, 1997.

The Law and Legislation of Credit cards, Irving J. Stone, London, Ocean Publications, 1987.

The Millionaire Next Door, Thomas J. Stanley and William D. Dankey, Longstreet Press, Marietta, GA, 1996.

Surviving the Squeeze, Stephen M. Pollan and Mark Levine, Collier Books, McMillan Publishing Company, 1994.

What Every Credit card User Needs to Know, Howard Strong, Henry Holt & Company, New York, 1992.

Index

E

F

G

H

I

J

L

M

N

P

Q

R

S

T

U

V

W

About the Author

Steven N. Taieb

Steven N. Taieb has been practicing consumer bankruptcy law since 1985. He has helped over 5,000 people deal with financial problems over the last 17 years. He is one of ten attorneys in New Jersey who are Board Certified in Consumer Bankruptcy Law by the American Board of Certification.

The requirements for board certification require passing a written exam, handling a large amount of consumer bankruptcy matters, plus concentrating your practice in consumer bankruptcy law. The certification also requires 20 hours of continuing legal education per year.

Mr. Taieb has been producing quarterly newsletters, for his clients and other attorneys over the last seven years.